91 Years Down The Road
With Tom O'Donnell, Sr.

91 Years Down The Road
With Tom O'Donnell, Sr.

by
Tom O'Donnell, Sr.

Pearce Publishers, Inc.
Timonium, Maryland, USA
1-800-662-2354
2003

91 Years Down The Road With Tom O'Donnell, Sr.
by Tom J. O'Donnell, Sr.

Copyright © 2003 by Tom J. O'Donnell, Sr. All rights reserved.
No part of this publication may be reproduced, stored in a retrieval system, or transmitted, in any form or by any means, electronic, mechanical, photocopying, recording, or otherwise, without the prior written permission of the copyright holder.

Cover Photo Courtesy of Maryland Department, Enoch Pratt Free Library

PEARCE PUBLISHERS, INC.
Timonimum, Maryland, USA
1-800-662-2354
2003
Printed in the United States of America

ISBN 1-883122-23-6

Publisher's Cataloging-in-Publication
(Provided by Quality Books, Inc.)

O'Donnell, Tom, Sr.
  91 years down the road with Tom O'Donnell, Sr. / by Tom O'Donnell, Sr.
  p. cm.
  ISBN 1-883122-23-6

  1. O'Donnell, Tom, Sr. 2. Journalists--United States --Biography. 3. Sun (Baltimore, Md. : 1837) 4. Public relations consultants--United States--Biography. 5. D'Alesandro, Thomas, 1903-1987. 6. Mayors--Maryland--Baltimore--Biography. I. Title.

PN4874.O475A3 2003   070'.92
                            QBI33-923

TABLE OF CONTENTS

Introduction	1
On To Hampden	2
Pretty Child?	2
Struggle for Existence	2
A Jewel of a Job	8
Little Italy's Boy	10
Tommy Goes to Work	12
Legislature Days	13
A Real Change of Life	15
Learning to Write	16
Fleming, Great City Editor	18
Golf After Midnight	20
A Busted Romance	21
A Golfing Judge	22
Wow, Mr. President	26
On To Eastern Shore	27
A Crisis Foiled	28
More Days in Sun	29
The Bricker Campaign	30
A Carrier Takeoff	32
Off To War	35
Meeting The Marines	36

Hiroshima Bombed! 37
Singing Marines 38
Japanese Reaction 39
The Emperor's Decision 40
American War Prisoners 41
Fun in Tokyo 43
The Lost Colony 44
Homeward Bound 45
Off To Puerto Rico 46
Another Life Change 47
Reporting Improvements 52
PGA Tourney for Baltimore 55
The Civic Center 58
School Children at City Hall 65
Political Ads 67
For Better Teeth 71
New Traffic Czar 72
Censorship! 76
The Return from Elba 81
Election A Big Success 84
Garbage Strike 84
Two Toms Reunited 88
Tommy Makes a Hit 88

ACKNOWLEDGEMENTS

Many thanks to those who helped and encouraged me to write these recollections of by-gone days:

Gail O'Donnell
Richard Lidinsky
William Zorzi
Michelle Roberts
Pat Thomas
Mary O'Donnell
Melanie Dorian
Thomas D'Alesandro, 3rd
Jane Sides

Special thanks to the star of this scenario, the late Mayor Thomas D'Alesandro, Jr., who, in my opinion, was the greatest mayor Baltimore has ever had.

INTRODUCTION

This is the story of two Baltimore boys growing up in poverty, one in Hampden and the other in Little Italy.

The one in Hampden, with a very sketchy self education, becomes a newspaper reporter and war correspondent during a 16-year career with the *Baltimore Sun* and then goes on to 10 years as public relations director of Baltimore City and as advisor and press spokesman for Mayor Thomas D'Alesandro, Jr., one of the most productive and popular mayors in the history of Baltimore.

The boy from Little Italy, also handicapped by poverty and little formal education, was, of course, the same Thomas D'Alesandro, Jr.

"Tommy" took the political road to great success through election to the Maryland House of Delegates, the Baltimore City Council and the United States House of Representatives where he earned the friendship of Presidents Franklin D. Roosevelt and Harry Truman, before becoming a three-term mayor of Baltimore.

Through a chance encounter in 1949 these two boys, now grown men, initiated a very close association that continued for many years through highs and lows, victories and defeats.

The boy from Hampden, yours truly, started out in life in South Baltimore where I was born on September 9, 1911, the fourth child in a family of 4 boys and 2 girls. My parents were Frank and Nan Brady O'Donnell.

My father, a big handsome man, had five brothers and two sisters. Two of his brothers became medical doctors and a third was the Southern police district magistrate for many years.

One of my cousins, William, had a distinguished legal career as states attorney, circuit court judge, and as a justice on the Maryland Court of Appeals.

Another cousin, Louis, was a top political writer for the Baltimore Sun and then became chief of staff for Maryland Governor William Preston Lane, Jr.

Although my father, Frank, attended college he apparently was more interested in playing baseball than in higher learning. He settled for a career in the U.S. Postal Service.

His father was a steamboat engineer who came to this country from Ireland when he was 15 years old.

My mother was a native of Martinsburg, West Virginia and one of four daughters of a Baltimore and Ohio Railroad engineer. He was transferred to Baltimore and that is where she met and married my father.

ON TO HAMPDEN

I was 2 years old when we moved to Hampden where my father was to reign as the postmaster for some years. We lived in a duplex two-story brick house only three blocks from the post office and virtually next door to St. Thomas Aquinas Church, school and Convent. Our house, like most of the others in the neighborhood, had gaslights, back yard privies, a coal burning stove in the parlor and a wood stove in the kitchen. There were none of today's treasures like washing machines, TV's or even radios, nothing electric, no telephone.

We did have a hand-cranked record player called a "Victrola" on which we played records featuring Caruso and John McCormick, and we also had an old upright piano.

PRETTY CHILD?

To my sometimes mortification I was regarded as a "pretty child" and my mother had me wearing curls until I was 5 years old.

Just up the street from our house on Union Avenue, at the corner of Roland Avenue, was the Hampden fire engine house and the firemen, who didn't have too much to do, would sit outside and carve little wooden toys for the neighborhood kids. The story is told that the firemen would tease me, calling me a little girl and that I would take down my pants and prove that I wasn't.

Life for some years was uneventful. My three brothers and I were all altar boys at St. Thomas and I was frequently called on to serve the 5 AM "Workmen's mass" and to serve funeral masses and ride in the limousine with the priest to the cemetery. Those limo rides were pretty heady stuff for a kid whose family, like most of their neighbors, had no automobile.

To augment family income, since post office pay was meager, the two older boys in our family, Frank and Bill, became caddies, at the Baltimore Country Club in Roland Park. There was no stigma attached to that because nearly all of the boys in Hampden were caddies, as the area was a working men's district with most families hovering around the poverty line.

STRUGGLE FOR EXISTENCE

Then, when I was 9 years old, on the night after Christmas, tragedy struck our family. My father recently had been transferred to the main post office downtown and shortly after he had left the building he suffered a massive heart attack, collapsed and died. He was only 46 years old.

My mother, then 42 years old, was left with a mortgage, six children and very little else. The oldest child, Frank, was 15; my sister Victoria, was 14; William was 12; as mentioned, I was 9; John was 7 and our little sister, Sarah (Sally) was only 3.

Then began a struggle for existence. In 1920 there was no such thing as public assistance and even if there had been, we were too proud to have accepted it.

My mother was the best and bravest mother imaginable. She had to face a very precarious future and she did so with a brave heart and unwavering spirit. Without delay she obtained a night shift job as a timekeeper at one of the Mount Vernon cotton mills in nearby Woodberry.

After preparing dinner and putting it on the table for us she would go to our old upright piano and play us a little concert to keep up our spirits while we ate. Then she would head off to her job at the mill. Fortunately, there was a little "Toonerville Trolley" line nearby that ran to the mill area.

Meanwhile, my brother Frank got a job with R.G. Dun & Co., a credit rating company, and started a lengthy night school program that carried him through high school and college to an executive position in sales and management with the Denison Manufacturing Company. My sister, Victoria, pretended to be a stenographer, lied about her age and learned how on the job, later switching to employment in a department store beauty salon.

A couple of years later Bill got a job with the gas and electric company, spent many years in night school and became an accountant.

Sally grew up, married and mothered a son and five daughters.

My brother John and I took different routes as time went on. John became a caddy, of course, and at the age of 16, became assistant to the golf professional at the Green Spring Valley Hunt Club. John went on to become a top-flight golf professional, won five Virginia Open championships, two Maryland open titles and played in numerous national opens and PGA championships. Always a club pro, he was inducted in the Middle Atlantic Golf Hall of Fame.

My own experience as a caddy actually began at the age of 8 and was limited to just a few outings that year. When you were assigned to a job by the caddy master that was called "getting out." Sometimes when there were few players and many caddies you could go a whole summer day and not "get out."

I can hardly believe it myself but I started smoking secretly, when I was only 8 years old. My father smoked "Recruits," little cigars the size of cigarettes. They would go out as soon as put down so there were always butts to find around the house. They were so strong they made cigarettes seem mild.

All the caddies smoked. We were not above picking up butts from the street and smoking them. Cigarettes yes, but drugs, no way. My mother told us that the most horrible thing that could happen to anyone was to become a "dope fiend" as drug addicts were then called. Not "substance abusers," but dope fiends.

To get to the Baltimore Country Club it was a walk of only a mile or so. Although you could ride the trolley line for just a nickel, Hampden kids walked. A nickel was a nickel.

The clubhouse was located in ritzy Roland Park as were the 1st, 17th and 18th holes of their beautiful old course. The other 15 holes were on a tract of land on the west side of Falls Road where a couple of public high schools are today.

The first tee and the clubhouse were at the top of a steep hill. A little way down the hill were several long benches in the shade of large trees and these were the caddy quarters. There the kids, sometimes as many as 30 or more, played cards or other games waiting to be called by name for a job by the caddy master who in that era was Leo Kernan. Caddies were divided into three classes. "A" class was older and more experienced. They were paid 60 cents, plus tip, for the job of carrying their player's bag, finding the ball when shots went astray and sometimes giving advice. "B" class, less experienced, got 40 cents plus tip, and "C" class were the little kids, beginners, 30 cents.

For me, caddying was not a hardship. Every caddy I knew became a golfer and every year the club held a caddy tournament for us, the players lending their clubs to the kids. Not only that, for years all the caddies were treated to a weekly visit to a big downtown theater that had feature films and five acts of live vaudeville, every Tuesday evening. One of the club members, a Mr. Whitehurst, owned the theater on Lexington Street and he arranged that all the caddies were admitted by a blanket pass carried by caddy master Kernan, whose nickname to the kids was "Oogy." All the kids in the Hampden area would ride the #10 trolley car downtown and gather outside the theater by 7 P.M. We would all be milling around and then there would be a shout, "Here comes Oogy." In a jiffy we would go thundering up the stairs to the balcony. More often than not I would get sick going home on the trolley car from the smell of the electric engine and throw up out the back window.

Another highlight of the caddying days occurred during the city's annual "Boys Week" observance. This included a banquet in a downtown hotel where poor boys were the guests of prominent civic leaders, including the Mayor. My brother Bill and I were the guests of Robert Worthington and Louis Windholz, for whom we often caddied. It was quite a thrill when a big new Buick pulled up in front of our house and took us off to the banquet. Talk about Cinderella!

Another caddy plus, the country club had 8 or 10 grass tennis courts in those days, and as a little kid I had the opportunity to see the great Bill Tilden play an exhibition tennis match against Bill Johnson and to see Davis Cup matches between Japan and Australia. Playing for Australia were Pat O'Hara Wood and Gerald Patterson. One of the Japanese players I can remember was Takeichi Harada.

Additionally, I had the privilege of being a "fore caddy" in a match played by the legendary Bobby Jones and his Atlanta amateur partner, Watts Gunn, against the Corkran brothers B. Warren and W. Clarke, who represented the country club. The match ended in a tie.

But another caddy memory that I will never forget occurred on July 4 when I was 12 years old. The day before, James R. Edmunds, a prominent Baltimore architect, a player for whom I often caddied, told me that he and his golfing partner, a dentist named Mitchell, were going to play on the Fourth at 5 A. M. and would I caddy for them. I agreed and we completed the round by 8 A.M.

Because of the national holiday caddies were scarce so the caddy master asked me if I was ready to go out again. I agreed and was assigned to carry the bags of two men in a foursome.

By 1 P.M. that round was completed and I was getting ready to head for home when the caddy master asked if I thought I could make another round. I said I didn't know about that, I had gotten up too early for breakfast and I hadn't any lunch. One of the players spoke up and said I will get you some lunch and so he did. He went into the clubhouse and came back with two chicken sandwiches and a tall glass of milk.

The players waited until I finished the lunch and off we went for my third round carrying two bags.

Now golf bags in those days were not as big as they are now and had fewer clubs in them. Nevertheless, the course was somewhat hilly

A pretty child? Nah! Author at age 4.

Author's mother, Nan Brady O'Donnell, who kept the family together and successfully raised them all.

Frank O'Donnell, Jr. and Frank, Sr. Young Frank was 15 years old and his father, Frank, Sr. was 46 when this photo was taken, just a few months before the elder died of a heart attack.

The four O'Donnell boys. From left, William, John, Frank and author.

and the 18th hole was straight up a steep hill. So, walking 54 holes was really a grind for a skinny kid.

There was a "tea garden" on a plateau overlooking the 18th green where stylishly dressed men and women sipped tea or illegal cocktails, and off to one side there was a string trio playing classical music. It was the most welcoming sound imaginable as I struggled up the hill that late afternoon.

Just consider. Walking three rounds carrying double and earning a total of $6, a really big sum in the 1920's ... That was a day to remember and I still do nearly 80 years later.

Things were so tough financially in those early years after my father's death that once or twice the evening meal depended on "getting out" at the golf course.

A JEWEL OF A JOB

But I'm getting a little ahead of myself. When I was 11, I got a job after school and on Saturday at the jewelry store of E. Arthur Newman on 36th street in Hampden. This was during the winter months. I saw a sign in the window "boy wanted" so I went in, said I was 14 and got the job at $5 a week. My job included sweeping up and washing the big front window, but my main responsibility was to carry diamonds to be reset and watches to be repaired downtown by trolley car to a manufacturing jeweler named John A. Tschantre on East Baltimore Street.

The jewelry store job went along fine for a couple of months until a woman in the neighborhood went to Mr. Newman and told him he could get in trouble hiring an 11 year old kid. That ended that.

The following winter I got a job as a soda jerk in a drug store and it ended in pretty much the same fashion.

I can't remember when or how I learned to read but I certainly loved it. There was and still is a lovely little public library branch in the 3600 block of Falls Road only three blocks from our home. From the time I was 7 and until I was grown I spent many a winter afternoon or evening in that library reading any and everything that came to hand. Among the books I devoured were The Rise and Fall of the Roman Empire, The Conquest of Mexico, Crime and Punishment, Moby Dick, the works of Dickens, Shakespeare, Julius Caesar and all of Kipling's stories about India. Indiscriminately, I read fiction, histories, books on art and famous classical artists. I had, through the enjoyment of reading, knowledge of the world and the countries in it that most kids had not.

To illustrate, when I was in the fifth grade at St. Thomas, the nun who was teaching the class was telling stories about renowned figures of the distant past, including Alexander the Great. Pausing, she asked, does anyone in the class know the name of Alexander's famous horse? There was silence and then I put up my hand and said, "Bucephalus."

The teacher asked, how did you know that? I told her that I had a big book at home on ancient history which I enjoyed reading.

That little incident led to my skipping from the 5th to the 7th grade with some private tutoring by my teacher. This resulted in my graduating from grammar school at the age of 13.

When I was in the 7th grade I took up running as a sport. In those days in Baltimore there was an organization known as the Playground Athletic League (PAL) sponsored by civic organizations and the Police Department. The organization, among other endeavors, put on street races and track and field events in the various neighborhoods. In the Hampden area there was a large water department reservoir shaped like the capital letter D. It was located in a small park named after Teddy Roosevelt just west and south of Falls Road and 36th Street. The circumference of the reservoir had been measured at just a few feet less than a half mile and the straight line part was an ideal place to have a cinder track for 100 yard and 220 yard dashes while a complete circuit of the reservoir was just right for half mile runs.

I competed in a number of street runs. Many of the runners were men and I would finish anywhere from 15th to 25th.

However, I did better in track meets at Roosevelt Park, consistently winning the half-mile races. Doing a half-mile was easy as pie for me because I gradually lengthened the distance I could run until I could make 20 circuits around the reservoir, ten miles. I was just at an age when body changes were occurring and I developed a big chest. This was helpful when, while still only 13, I applied for a job at the Maryland Casualty Insurance Company located only a half dozen blocks from our home, now at 3714 Roland Avenue, to which we recently had moved. On the application form I put down my age as 16 and when the company doctor examined me he remarked that I had a very well developed chest for a boy of 16. My job was as a mail boy and I was an assistant to an old gentleman who smoked cigars and was fond of saying that he couldn't hustle like he used to. Before long he was giving me a cigar every day. Since I had been smoking for about 5 years moving to cigars was no big deal. It was at the Maryland Casualty Company that I met my future wife, Florence Reich, a very pretty brunette who was only 17 and I, 18 at the time.

But while I was growing up in Hampden, what was occurring with the boy from Little Italy?

LITTLE ITALY'S BOY

A formal biography would recount that Thomas D'Alesandro, Jr. was born on August 1, 1903, the son of Thomas and Mary Antoinette (Foppiano) D'Alesandro. His father was born in Abruzzi, Italy and came to the United States when he was 20 years old. Young Tommy's mother was born in Baltimore.

The D'Alesandros had 13 children and the father worked as a laborer for the city and often held two jobs to feed and shelter his growing family.

Young Tommy attended St. Leo's parochial school adjacent to the D'Alesandro home and was an altar boy at St. Leo's church.

As he noted years later, life was a struggle to make ends meet. His father for a time operated a small grocery store in East Baltimore but had to close it down when many of his customers couldn't pay their bills. During World War One the senior D'Alesandro worked a second job at night at the Bartlett Hayward munitions plant.

Like the boy in Hampden, young Tommy first earned income at the age of 8, working for orthodox Jewish neighbors as a "Shabbas Goy," the term literally meaning "Sabbath Gentile." He recalled that devout Jews strictly observed the Sabbath from Friday evening to Saturday evening and would not even do such things as turn on a stove, or light a candle or open an envelope. They employed a Shabbas Goy for this.

In memoirs dictated to my tape recorder, Mr. D'Alesandro said, "Although I was an altar boy at St. Leo's Church, I saw nothing wrong in serving as a Shabbas Goy. I used to perform little duties for these Jewish families and earned a little money."

He also spoke of another way the kids in the neighborhood could make a little money. In those days, he said, there were some "sporting houses" on Caroline street and when you went along there you could see men lined up to go in. For a long time he thought they were bathhouses. The kids, he said, used to buy chewing gum for 3 packs for a dime and sometimes sell it to the girls at the windows for as much as a quarter.

Although years later, in 1954, he was an essential factor in bringing big league baseball back to Baltimore after an absence of 50 years, he liked to talk about a baseball team he helped organize when just a kid in the neighborhood. He and other boys scraped together a few old gloves and bats but were lacking in uniforms, he said. Determined to look as much like a real baseball player as possible, he filched a pair of an older sister's long drawers and wore them as baseball knickers. When she happened to come by their "field," which was a vacant lot, she spotted him and her drawers and chased him faster than any trip he ever made around the bases.

Another time he got in trouble over baseball "pants' was the day he sneaked the trousers of his father's Sunday suit out of the house and put them on, using garters to bag them up around the knees in approved knickers fashion. Running for second base in a game that morning he forgot what he was wearing and slid into the bag, putting a big rip in the pants. A couple of plays later he got hit in the eye by a bounding ball, so he went home with a black eye and torn pants. "I was expecting a good whipping from my father," he recalled, but his father felt sorry for him because of his black eye, although the parent had to miss church the next day while the pants were being repaired.

St. Leo's Parochial School, which young Tommy attended for 8 years, minus two weeks, was the source of most of his formal education. Sister Pauline, he said, was the principal and a wonderful woman. She taught the 5th, 6th, 7th and 8th grades in the same room at the same time. He noted that the classes were very small, and that when he was in the eighth grade there were only four boys and one girl in the class.

During his last year at St. Leo's he won a spelling bee and Sister Pauline pinned a big medal of the Blessed Virgin on him and said he could wear it for a week. At recess time one of the boys in his class "gave him the razzberry" as a sissy for wearing the medal, so he picked up a rock and threw it at him, cutting his head. Sister Pauline saw what happened and not only took the medal away from him and boxed his ears, she also told him to bring his father to school the next morning.

He was afraid to tell his father or mother about the incident so the next day Sister Pauline wanted to know where his father was. The first thing he could think of was to say that his father was ill with pleurisy and couldn't come. That seemed to satisfy the school principal but the next morning she saw Mrs. D'Alesandro at early mass and told her that she was praying for Mr. D'Alesandro's recovery. When the latter looked at Sister Pauline with a question in her eyes, the nun wanted to know how her husband was. Why he is just fine, Mrs. D'Alesandro replied, I saw him off to work just before coming to church.

Sister Pauline didn't let the prevaricating student forget that day in a hurry. As a matter of fact, he recalled in later years, Sister Pauline got so fed up with him and the other three boys in the class over a series of incidents that she expelled all four of them just two weeks before they were to graduate. Many years later when the erstwhile student had become a congressman the sisters of St. Leo's set up a ceremony in the school yard and presented him with a diploma at last.

TOMMY GOES TO WORK

After leaving St. Leo's the future friend of presidents went to work for a sawmill that was making ammunition boxes for use in England and France, which were heavily involved in World War I. The place where he went to work was called the Union Box Factory and the men who operated saws were paid $8.80 per week. Boys picking up the cut wood and stacking it got only $6.60. He was one of the boys. Going on strike, the saw operators were raised to $9.90 a week but the mill owners thought they would balance things by reducing the boys' pay $1.10 a week. The boys promptly went on strike and not only got their $6.60 back but a raise to $7.70.

As a little kid, young D'Alesandro also worked for a while at the world famous McCormick spice plant on Light Street. He was in the powdered mustard department. He recalled the workplace was very hot and all that powdered mustard in the air made his skin swell up with big blisters.

Years later, at a big dinner of industrialists, among them Charles P. McCormick, president of the spice company, Mr. D'Alesandro, then a congressman, decided to have some fun. So, when it was his turn to speak he said," I am very proud tonight to be seated next to my employer of long, long ago, Mr. Charles P. McCormick, who paid me the handsome sum of 12 and a half cents an hour for picking fly specks out of pepper while wearing boxing gloves. That really broke up the businessmen all of whom knew and liked Charley McCormick, who had been an outstanding civic leader in Maryland for many years. "In fact, I got such a hand with that joke that I used it many times in later years whenever Charley McCormick was present, although he used to beg me not to do that again," Mr. D'Alesandro said.

"Charley was president of the Board of Regents at the University of Maryland for many years and when I became Mayor I was happy to appoint him chairman of the Baltimore Civic Center Commission that planned and built Baltimore's convention hall and indoor sports arena."

Getting back to memories of his youth, "Tommy" recalled that he was less than 14 years of age when he went to work as an office boy at the Harry T. Poor Insurance Agency and it was his first "white collar" job. "I'll always remember going to work at the insurance agency. Mr. Poor offered me $6 a week but I held out for $7. He wanted to know why and I told him it would be a dollar a day for the six days I worked, plus a dollar spending money for me. He laughed and put me on at $7. "I continued to work there all through my youth. When I was 21 they gave me a chance to sell insurance on a contract calling for an annual quota. I exceeded the quota by 500% the first year," he recalled.

"Growing up in "Little Italy" was not the most exciting life in the world although when prohibition went into effect the area had its share of bootleggers and speakeasies. That didn't mean anything to me because of a pledge I had taken to abstain from drinking until I was 35," he said.

"As a teenager, I was very active in church affairs at St. Leo's, participating in plays put on by a drama group, helping to run the annual parish street carnival and especially, organizing parish dances. I always considered myself a pretty smooth dancer," he continued.

Before the future congressman, mayor, etc. reached voting age he had had a taste or two of politics giving out campaign literature and helping to get out the vote.

By the time he was 21 years old, his popularity was such that he was put up as a candidate for the Maryland House of Delegates, thus starting a 50-year political career that saw 22 consecutive election victories.

He often said later that his first victory came about through a petition he drew up recommending him to voters that he carried from door to door in the district and which garnered 500 signatures.

LEGISLATURE DAYS

Recounting his first day at the Legislature he said he was all dressed up with patent leather shoes, an oxford gray suit, a polka dot bow tie, spats and a derby. He said he thought he would encounter men of the stature of Thomas Jefferson, Patrick Henry and the like and felt let down when he saw that his legislative associates were just ordinary citizens you could see anywhere.

Young D'Alesandro served as a member of the House of Delegates for 7 years, was a member of the Baltimore City Council for 4 years, and then was elected to the first of 5 terms in congress before progressing to 12 years as probably the most productive and popular mayor in the city's history.

Mr. D'Alesandro was married at the age of 25 on September 30, 1928 to Annunciata (Nancy) Lombardi. Their children included Thomas, 3rd, who also became a mayor of Baltimore, and sons Franklin D, Nicholas, Hector and Joseph. Their only daughter, (now Nancy Pelosi), is the first woman in history to be elected minority leader in the U.S. Congress. She was elected to this post by the Democratic party members of the House.

Thomas D'Alesandro, Jr.'s career could serve as an inspiration to any boy from a family in straitened financial circumstances. Not daunted by his limited formal education, he became "Tommy" to presidents, to the mayors of all the important cities in the country and to a host of other greats and near greats.

An even greater accomplishment was his ultimate conquest of the periodic bouts of depression, which plagued his adult years from time to time. His ailment was sometimes described as nervous exhaustion. Now it is known as "bipolar disorder."

Getting back to Hampden for a moment or two, life for me at the Maryland Casualty Company was mostly on the pleasant side. The company had several clay tennis courts on the grounds and Florence and I spent many evenings and weekends playing tennis.

Florence became secretary to a company vice president, Richard H. Thompson, who became my opponent in two of the company golf tournaments, and I advanced to a clerkship and then senior clerk in the rating and manuals division.

But things went sour when the stock market crashed in 1929 and the Great Depression followed. The Maryland Casualty had insured the mortgages on thousands of "second homes" in Florida being purchased by people all over the country. Many hundreds defaulted on their mortgages and the insurance company had to pay off the debts and take over the houses, which nobody could buy.

Company employees had to take two sizable pay cuts and the company was hovering on bankruptcy when I received a telephone call that changed my whole life.

A REAL CHANGE OF LIFE

It was from my cousin, Louis O'Donnell, then the Baltimore Sun's leading Maryland political writer. Louis told me that the newspaper was going to hire two police district news reporters and that if I were interested he could get me an interview with the Sun's managing editor, William E. Moore.

I jumped at the chance and went the next day to the Sun building, then at Baltimore and Charles Streets, for the interview. To reach Mr. Moore's office I had to pass through the big newsroom where several young fellows were banging away at typewriters.

Mr. Moore, a small resolute man with a limp dating back to World War I, greeted me pleasantly and got right down to business. He said, "What makes you think you can be a news reporter?"

"Are those young fellows out there in the big room news reporters?" I asked.

"Yes, they are," he said.

"If those fellows can be reporters so can I," was my reply.

Mr. Moore laughed heartily and said go down to the second floor and tell the treasurer that I said to put you on the payroll as a police district reporter.

Then he concluded without asking a word about education or anything else. Neither did anyone then or in the future make such an inquiry.

The second police district reporter hired that week, we were the first to be hired in several years, was Nat Kenney, a recent Princeton graduate. He worked for the paper many years and wound up at the National Geographic magazine.

My first day as a newspaper reporter was a day to remember. Here I was, 21 years old, just hired the day before at the munificent sum of $18 a week and assigned to the Southern police district. I was strictly on my own without a clue as to what to do or how to go about my new job. One of the Sun's veteran reporters was to have broken me in, but a family crisis made him unavailable and because the staff was short handed due to the depression, this was 1933, there was no one else to take me in hand. So the day city editor said just go ahead, you'll be all right.

There was one bright spot, however, my uncle, Joe O'Donnell, was a police court magistrate and his stomping ground happened to be the Southern police district court.

I found the police station house without too much difficulty, went on in and was looking things over when a policeman behind a big desk asked if he could help me.

After telling him I was a new reporter and giving him my name, the desk sergeant, for that is what he turned out to be, pointed to a table and chair over in a corner and said they were for the use of reporters along with the telephone. Then he went back to work.

Wandering around the big room I noticed an open door and a sign on it saying Captain William J. Forrest, District Commander. With the thought that news reporters had to look for news I went on in the empty office and was trying to read some reports on the Captain's desk when I heard a roar behind me.

Sure enough, it was Captain Forrest and he was shouting, "Who in the hell are you and what the hell are you doing in my office?" He went on reading the riot act while I was stuttering a reply. At this juncture a man appeared at the door and said,"Hi, Tom, what are you doing down here?" The man was my Uncle Joe, the district magistrate.

"Captain," said my uncle, "let me introduce my nephew, Tom O'Donnell."

"I was just welcoming him to the district," said the captain with a big smile.

Actually, Captain Forrest and I became good friends later on.

Police district reporters at the Sun went on duty at 3 P.M and covered district court hearings, accidents, fires, hold-ups, shootings and anything unusual that might be going on. We got off at 12 midnight.

For transportation we were given a supply of trolley car tokens. Fortunately, shortly before I started at the Sun I had saved enough to buy, for $100.00, a 1929 Ford convertible coupe complete with a "rumble seat" in the back. I bought it from the press agent for the downtown Century Theater. It was the first car in our family.

The first week I had it I took my mother and sister, Victoria, for a ride in the then rural Baltimore County. Before we got back I had to repair and pump up a couple of flat tires.

I used the Ford for several years in my work. The trolley car tokens were saved up and at the end of each month were taken to the car company's headquarters and turned in for cash, augmented income, as it were.

LEARNING TO WRITE

One of the most rewarding rules at the Sun was the requirement that police district reporters had to come in to the newsroom at 6 P.M.

and write reports on every item of interest that we had picked up since 3 P.M., whether it was a police court hearing, a fire, an accident or whatever. The reports were to be short, descriptive and accurate.

After that we grabbed a bite to eat and went back on duty until midnight. Any news events during the evening were to be telephoned into the city desk. A rewrite man would ask questions until he got the whole story.

The next morning when we read the Sun ... we looked anxiously for any items we had handled, especially the ones we had written. Such items were read closely to see what changes had been made at the city editor's desk, or at the copy desk where it was checked before it went down to the pressroom to be set in type.

Over the ensuing months the changes made it clear what the newspaper wanted and expected to get. Before long, the cub reporter learned to write acceptable copy and was on his way.

After a year or so of covering a wide variety of happenings, a young district reporter was "brought in" and promoted to general assignments.

My early general assignments were varied. Once I had to cover the wedding at midnight on New Year's Eve of a deaf mute couple who were surrounded by men and women friends with the same handicap. I got the necessary information with a pad and pencil.

On another occasion I was sent to cover the Timonium Fair and I went by train from the old Calvert Street station where the Sun papers building is now located. It was the first time I was ever on a train. In future years I twice crossed the country by train and made numerous shorter trips by steam, diesel and electric trains.

One of my first general assignments turned out to be something special. On a cold February evening about 7PM, I was told to take a cab and hustle down to the Coast Guard cutter's dock. The cutter Apache was going to rescue some watermen whose boats were frozen solid in bay ice. They shoved an old "Speed Graphic" camera under my arm and said get some pictures if you can.

When I reached the Apache, which was under the command of a young ensign named Polakias, I found that Jack Kavanaugh of the News Post was already aboard.

We got underway in a few minutes and after a couple of hours began to encounter thick ice. The Apache was pretty old for that kind of work but we kept battering along until dawn when we began to sight a number of oyster boats frozen tight.

The Apache would circle a boat as closely as safety would permit and toss a line to the watermen aboard and then tow the boat away.

It was hard grueling work, but one after another the cutter had a half dozen boats broken out and following us in a line like a mother duck and her brood toward Smith Island, the home base of the watermen.

Although I didn't know anything about how to use a speed graphic camera, I saw it had a plate in it so I went up on deck and by the dumbest luck imaginable got a very good picture of the boats trailing us into port. It ultimately was used on the front page of the Sun and I was given name credit for the photo.

Jack Kavanaugh and I got stories off to our papers using the cutter's radio to the Baltimore harbor master's office and we thought we might soon be heading home. Not to be. The Apache began getting one radio message after another reporting groups of watermen frozen in. They were from Crisfield, Tangier Island and other localities. Kavanaugh and I had nothing with us but the clothes we were wearing, not even a toothbrush. One day followed another and we were getting farther south until we finally reached Norfolk. I called the Sun and was told to stick with the Apache. On the other hand, Kavanaugh was told by the News Post to come on back. As a courtesy he agreed to take my camera and plate to the Sun with the result that my picture was published a couple of days before I got back.

Not long after my promotion to general assignments I was befriended by the city editor, H.K. Fleming, an Englishman, who was an avid golfer. When he learned I could play passably well, he invited me to play with him and a couple of older newsmen several mornings a week.

The country was still in the grip of depression and the owner of the Bonnie View Golf Club, a Mr. George R. Morris, made a deal with the Sun golfers, there were about 30 of us, which permitted us to play on weekdays for the whole summer for about $35 each.

FLEMING, GREAT CITY EDITOR

Fleming was very protective of his reporters. When an evening was quiet, news wise, he would quietly go to 2 or 3 reporters sitting around and say, "Would you like to see a cinema?" This was code for telling us to go off duty and get out of the newsroom.

He also was innovative. Responding to public unhappiness over slow traffic in Baltimore, he assigned reporters to take a bus; a trolley car; a taxicab; a bicycle; roller skates and finally a walker to see who could go fastest from Charles and Baltimore Streets to University Parkway and Charles. The bike rider won and the walker came in second.

When Pan American airways set up travel between Baltimore and Bermuda he assigned reporter Alfred Charles to go on the initial flight with his golf clubs, play 9 holes in Bermuda and then fly back and play the second 9 holes in Baltimore that same day to dramatize the new air service.

These were rollicking days for a single young fellow working as a news reporter. When we finished the work day not long after midnight there sometimes were all night poker games played on the desk of Jesse Linthicum, the Sports Editor, or a trip to the Oasis Cabaret on the notorious "Block" where reporters drank with the owner, Max Cohen, at the service bar at the back.

Another favorite after hours retreat was the "Fioretta Club" in Little Italy where the hospitality extended far beyond the legal closing hour of 2 a.m.

The Fioretta was often patronized by movie and stage personalities, including John Barrymore who periodically came to Baltimore to visit a young daughter then a student at a private Catholic school.

On one occasion, just for a gag, I had a waiter carry a note to Mr. Barrymore at the bar supposedly from a young woman at a corner table saying she would love to meet him. The joke backfired. The last time I saw old John that evening he was sitting at the table with the young woman and they were getting along famously.

A sometime visitor to the Sun was the famous boxing champion, Jack Dempsey. On this occasion, several years after he had been champion, he was sitting at Jesse Linthicum's desk chatting away. I got down on my hands and knees and, watched by an interested audience, crawled among the desks, slipped a match in the edge of the former champ's shoe and lit it off. I was safely away before Jack got the "hot foot". Dempsey let out a yell and jumped up from his chair and then joined in the laughter of the watchers. I went up and confessed that I was the perpetrator and apologized. He took it all in good humor and said he sometimes pulled practical jokes himself.

We had a celebrity of our own at the time. He was Lawrence Greene, author of "America Goes to Press," which recounted the greatest American news stories and "The Filabuster," a book about an American, William Walker, who took an "army" of about 400 men and successfully invaded Nicaragua. Walker ruled as dictator for several months but was defeated and overthrown.

GOLF AFTER MIDNIGHT

Lawrence Greene was a very chipper fellow who loved to play golf. He challenged me a couple of times but lost. Finally, he said he would play me for $5 but that he would name the conditions. I agreed so he stipulated that the match would be played at Bonnie View at 2 a.m. the following Sunday morning. A dozen or so Sun golfers turned out for the match, some carrying six packs of beer or other refreshments and a number had flashlights. Those with lights trooped out to both sides of the fairway on the first hole and yelled for us to tee off. We did and remarkably Greene and I kept our shots in the fairway until dawn finally arrived. Most of our gallery had drifted away before then and headed home. By the 13th hole Greene was behind by several shots and conceded the match.

We had another lively young reporter named Ralph Wallace. His father owned a newspaper, the Tiller and Toiler, in Larned, Kansas. Ralph was a graduate of the University of Kansas and had worked summers on his dad's paper. He was a top reporter and feature writer. He and his girlfriend, a student at the Peabody, and Florence and I made up a foursome to attend a new musical, "Roberta", the show that featured a big hit, "Smoke Gets in Your Eyes." The girls wore evening gowns, Ralph had on white tie and tails and I wore a tuxedo borrowed from the city editor. We had wangled the use of a box at Ford's Theater, the show's tryout was a hit and our evening was a great success. After the show we had a drink or two and then split up. I drove Florence to her home in Catonsville and then went home to bed.

About 4 o'clock in the morning I was rousted out of bed for a telephone call from Ralph. He evidently had gone on to the Fioretta Club after taking his girlfriend home and had gotten a "snoot full," as they used to say. He had fallen into the hands of the Central District police after an altercation at the club and he wanted me to get him out. I duly arrived at Central and was told they would let him go in my care if I took responsibility for him. The desk sergeant knew me and was doing me a favor. An officer was sent to bring Ralph out and Ralph really outdid himself this time. He came galloping into the main room of the police station neighing like a horse, his dress tails flying. "Take him back" shouted the desk sergeant, "he's still too drunk to let him go." So, I had to take a seat and wait. After about an hour the desk sergeant told an officer to take me back and see whether Ralph had quieted down. He had, so they let him go in my care, no charge.

It fell to my lot several years later to have a somewhat similar experience with Larry Greene. He had left the Sun and was connected with a publishing house in New York. He came down to visit his friends at the Sun and had some drinks with the boys. Sometime long after midnight I got a phone call. It was Larry. The police had picked him up on a drunk and disorderly charge and he wanted me to get him out. I got to the police station and gave them a sob story that Larry was an old Sun man in town for just a visit and that he would be returning to New York in the morning. They let him go in my care. He went back to New York and we never heard from him again.

A BUSTED ROMANCE

While I was kicking up my heels and thoroughly enjoying newspaper reporting, working at night and on Saturdays and Sundays, with days off in midweek, played havoc with my romance with Florence Reich. We saw less and less of each other and it led to quarrels that resulted in a complete break that lasted more than a year.

Ultimately, I realized that we belonged together so I telephoned her and asked if she would take me back. She said yes and we resumed the courtship. We were married in 1939 just a few days after Hitler invaded Poland. Our honeymoon was spent on a Merchant and Miner's steamship on a 10-day cruise to Miami and return at the very modest cost of $60 each. Our marriage lasted for 57 years, ending in 1997 when after a 3-year struggle against cancer, Florence died at the age of 84 years.

Florence was seldom involved in my newspaper work during our courtship. An exception occurred in 1936 when two Japanese warships visited Baltimore in the course of a worldwide training cruise. The two ships, both antiquated cruisers, had been active participants in the 1895 war against Russia. I was assigned to cover the Japanese ships for the entire week they were tied up in the Inner Harbor. This was five years before Pearl Harbor and friendly relations prevailed between the U.S. and Japan.

Early in the week I took a small group of the Japanese officers for a "night on the town" winding up in Councill's Bar, just a few steps away from the Old Sun Building, where they were served Kentucky style mint juleps. Returning the courtesy, the Japanese officers invited me to a luncheon aboard one of the cruisers and urged me to bring any friends I chose to join me. Naturally, I thought of Florence and also a long-time friend, Jimmy Hartzell, a Sun papers artist. A couple of other Sun people heard about it and asked if they could come along so our party was increased to five. The luncheon was held in the officer's wardroom and was quite enjoyable. Florence was given a beautiful fan as a souvenir.

Widening my experience I sometimes filled in as a court reporter in State and Federal Courts.

A GOLFING JUDGE

Believe it or not my caddying experiences were helpful even in court coverage. One of the Baltimore Circuit Court judges, W. Conwell Smith, was presiding in a case on which I needed some information. So, I went to see him. I remembered him as a golfer at the Baltimore Country Club who, as a young lawyer, once made a bet that he could "break ninety" using only a putter. In other words, he would shoot a round of 18 holes in less than 90 strokes using just one club and, by golly, he did. A tall, lanky man, he always used a putter with a shaft long enough for use as a driving iron. When I was admitted to his office, one of the first things I said to him was, "Judge, do you remember the day you broke 90 with a putter? How in the world would you know about that?" he asked. Then I told him I knew all about it as a caddy. He seemed very pleased and was quite helpful.

Something similar happened when I was covering a very complicated case in Federal court involving the reorganization of the Seaboard Airline Railroad. The company was in bankruptcy and there were at least six teams of lawyers representing groups of investors such as common and preferred stockholders, and representatives of various classes of bondholders. To add to the confusion, the case had been dragging on for several years under a Federal judge in Norfolk, VA, who unfortunately for everyone involved, suffered a fatal heart attack.

The case was removed to Baltimore and assigned to Judge W. Calvin Chesnut, for whom I had sometimes caddied on Sunday afternoons prior to his appointment to the Federal bench. Days were spent by the many lawyers arguing how their clients should share in the company's assets and in bringing Judge Chesnut up to date on what had gone on before. The arguments were so complicated that in an effort to make sure I was reporting accurately, I took a chance and telephoned Judge Chesnut at home on the first evening. I told him I was covering the case for the Sun and just happened to mention that I used to caddy for him years ago. He agreed the case was very complicated and graciously outlined the facts as he saw them and said he would be glad to help in the future. He was a fine judge and a real gentlemen.

Tom and Florence O'Donnell with friends "Sugar" McElgunn, Mary Clare and Bill Sullivan, out for an evening.

The author as a 23 year old reporter for the *Baltimore Sun*.

A youthful Tom O'Donnell in the then fashionable knickers.

Pre-Pearl Harbor. In 1936, author took a group of Japanese naval officers for a "night on the town" In Councill's Bar they tried mint juleps. Author is second from left.

The Japanese officers, from two cruisers that visited Baltimore, enjoyed their "night out" so much they invited the author to bring a group of friends to a luncheon on one of the cruisers. My girl friend and, later, wife for 57 years, Florence Reich, made a big hit with the Japanese.

The fact that I had learned short hand was very useful in coverage of court trials, especially on Q & A testimony of witnesses. One courthouse assignment led to a lot of work that ended with complete frustration. It was noticed at the Sun that a lot of lawbreakers seemed to be getting off with probation or dismissal for a wide variety of crimes. Neil Swanson, then executive editor of both the Evening Sun and the Sun, assigned me to go to the court house and study the docket of each of the various criminal courts for the last year and make notes on every case involving murder, holdups, burglary, rape, assault and other crimes of violence that seemed to reflect excessive leniency in sentencing. I spent every working day for six weeks studying the dockets and making copious notes. Everyone in the court house became aware of what I was doing. When I concluded the work, which actually wore calluses on my fingers, I reached the conclusion, submitted to Mr. Swanson, that in Baltimore you could get away with murder and virtually every other crime in the book, adding that I had numerous cases to support the conclusion.

In a day or two, after I had started to write a series of articles on the subject, I received word from the executive editor that the chief judge of the courts, then known as the Supreme Bench, had telephoned him to say that such a series of articles "would destroy the Supreme Bench" and requested that the articles be withheld, at the same time promising improvements in the operation of the courts. The executive editor said that reluctantly he had agreed to spike the articles.

A couple of years before that episode occurred, several momentous events happened. One was the tragic death of Paul Banker, the assistant managing editor, who drowned while swimming in the Chesapeake Bay. Our city editor, Fleming was moved up to fill that position and William Knighton was moved from the copy desk to become city editor. Subsequently, Mr. Moore, the man who hired me, retired and both Fleming and Knighton advanced another step up. Ed Young became city editor and I took Young's spot as assistant city editor.

But while all these things were going on at the Sun, how were things progressing with our young man from Little Italy?

WOW, MR. PRESIDENT!

As he told me and my tape recorder years later, things were great. He said: "Wow, Mr. President, if the boys in the old neighborhood could only see me now."

"I burst out, I couldn't help it," he continued.

"The scene was in the White House, the famous Oval Room office of President Franklin Delano Roosevelt, who then was in the full flower of his power and glory. The year was 1938. The country was coming out of the depression and the world was pretty much at peace. "A moment before, FDR had extended his silver cigarette case to me and I had nervously selected one, he held me a light with an engraved lighter. Out of respect, though, I made him light his own first and he chuckled at my exclamation as he did so. "Here I was, a freshman Congressman for the first time in private conversation with a President of the United States. In back of me were two terms in the Maryland State Legislature and a term in the Baltimore City council. But although I was to serve 5 terms in Congress and subsequently 12 years as Mayor of my hometown, Baltimore, numbering Presidents, senators, cabinet members and business tycoons as friends and associates, this was one of the most memorable occasions of my life. Me, the kid from Baltimore's Little Italy who missed getting his 8th grade diploma by two weeks, having his cigarette lighted by the president."

"Typically, I was in the President's office seeking patronage, as it is called, jobs for my constituents. Although I was voting 100 percent New Deal on all legislation, so far I hadn't been getting any jobs to hand out."

"FDR soon ended that situation, but more about that later. It really wasn't my first meeting with FDR. That had come a few months earlier on the Eastern Shore of Maryland where the President spoke at Denton as part of his effort to "purge" Maryland's Senator Millard Tydings, who was strongly anti-New Deal."

"I was running for Congress in a Democratic working-man's district in Baltimore but I attended because I had placed myself on the same ticket with Congressman Davy Lewis, of Western Maryland, who was FDR's primary election choice over Tydings, and I wanted to be as closely identified with the President as possible.

"In my district, Roosevelt was everyone's idol, as he was mine. In fact, one of my sons is named Franklin D. Roosevelt D'Alesandro and he was born the day the President took office in 1933."

"Young "Roosie,", as we called him, was all dressed up for the Denton affair and presented a basket of flowers to the President."

ON TO EASTERN SHORE

"I went to Denton with my whole family, my wife Nancy and all six children, and I was anxious to have a picture taken with the President. But as bad luck would have it, when I got to the head of the receiving line and was shaking hands with FDR the attention of all the newspaper photographers was diverted elsewhere. There was a little girl with a box camera standing nearby so I called to her to take the picture. I kept saying over and over again "I'm glad to meet you Mr. President" and while I was pumping away on his hand I kept yelling to the little girl, "snap the picture, snap the picture". "She did, finally, so I dropped the President's hand and ran over to the little girl. "She agreed, so we made the exchange, I gave her $20 for the camera. That night I took the camera back to Baltimore and hurried up to the Sun papers photographic department to have the picture developed. It was my hope, of course, to get it published and make good use of it for the rest of the campaign. But the picture was something of a disaster. I was shaking hands with the President all right, but all the Secret Service men had their hands on their pistols and were glaring at me like I was some sort of crank who might be intending the President bodily harm. Anyhow, the picture definitely was not suitable for campaign use and at my urging the newspaper didn't publish it."

"However, the most hilarious meeting I had with President Roosevelt came after I had become a Congressman and I saved him from what could have become a most embarrassing experience. On this occasion, FDR was in Maryland to visit the Glenn L. Martin aircraft plant where he was scheduled to make an efficiency award and a speech to pep up the morale of the defense workers. Helicopters weren't in general use in those days and the President was riding in an open car at the head of a motorcade. As the line of cars neared the Martin plant, the President ordered a stop by the roadside for a sort of picnic lunch in the cars. I was with a group in one of the following cars and I remember the State Police asking me, "What are you going to do, Tommy, eat the White House food or the State Police food? I said, "I'm going to eat the White House food, of course, and I did. While I was eating I noticed the White House provisions didn't include any coffee, so I walked over to the State Police and asked them to give me some of their coffee. The State Police said you're eating White House food, drink White House Coffee. When I said they didn't have any they said that's just too bad. Finally, though, they relented and gave me some."

A CRISIS FOILED

"It was after I had strolled back to the President's car that the nearly disastrous incident occurred. Among the others in the motorcade that day was the United States Marshal for Baltimore, Gus Klecka, and his wife, Lil, who were well known in local political circles. Lil was quite a politician herself and liked to be in on everything. So she decided it was a good opportunity during the lunch stopover to go up to the President's car and shake his hand. Well, it happened that one of the reasons the President had selected that particular spot was because he had to relieve his bladder. Physically handicapped as he was, he didn't want to get out of the car, so they got him an empty quart milk bottle. He was making good use of the bottle when Lil Klecka came puffing up toward the car. Knowing the President was in no position to receive ladies at the moment, I shouted a warning and grabbing Lil around the shoulders; I began waltzing her down the side of the road. She was furious at first but quickly caught on that something was awry. FDR appreciated my intervention and with his great sense of humor got a real kick out of the incident—when it was safely over, of course."

"President Roosevelt always was "boss" to me and I am proud to say that I was "Tommy" to him, as I was later to Presidents Truman, Kennedy and Johnson. Altogether I served in elective public office for 34 years and only by a very narrow margin did I miss election to the United States Senate, losing to an old friend and colleague, Republican Senator J. Glenn Beall. Until that hairline defeat in the 1958 election I had won 22 consecutive primary and general elections. Although I wasn't to win any more elections, subsequently I served more than eight years as a member of the Federal Renegotiation Board by appointment of President Kennedy and President Johnson. "Still later I served for nine years as a member of the Maryland State Parole Board."

MORE DAYS IN SUN

Turning again to the Hampden product, as the father of a child conceived before Pearl Harbor (my son, Tom Jr., was born on Feb. 5, 1942) I was deemed exempt from the draft, as was my cousin, Louis.

The war soon thinned the ranks of reporters at the Sun and in the Sun's Washington Bureau. A number of girls were hired as reporters, mostly inexperienced, and there were days when cousin Lou and I wrote virtually every local story in the papers. Frequently I was detailed to assignments in Washington that normally would have been covered by the Washington office.

In 1943 there was a change made in draft regulations that ended my deferment. I was ordered by the draft board to appear for physical examination and induction. At the armory I was checked by several doctors, passing with flying colors, and then came to my final doctor. As he was going about his work I said doctor I would like to call to your attention that I have a fistula, a pilonidol sinus. A fistula is located at the tip end of your spine and when aggravated can be extremely painful. Once, when I was driving to Cumberland on an assignment in Western Maryland, my fistula was acting up and so painful that I was practically standing up driving before I reached Cumberland. The doctor said, " Let me take a look at that." Then he said, "That's a fistula alright and it means you're out of here. The army has learned that soldiers with fistulas are more trouble than they are worth. They can't ride in tanks or jeeps and they are always needing medical treatment. So, you are rejected and you will be designated 4-F." So, instead of saving my rear end, my rear end saved me.

THE BRICKER CAMPAIGN

In 1944, during the hotly contested presidential election campaign between FDR, seeking a fourth term, and Tom Dewey, of New York, Dewey's running mate John W. Bricker complained to the Sun about coverage of his campaign. So, I was assigned to join up with Governor Bricker on his special campaign train where I spent the last six weeks of the campaign traveling through many mid-western and western states.

Every day was pretty much the same on the campaign train. There were many reporters aboard. We ate, slept and typed our stories as we rolled along. Our best friend on the train was Joe Brown, a Baltimorean, who worked for the Western Union Telegraph Company. To get your story to your paper each day all you had to do was turn it over to Joe Brown. He saw to it that your copy reached its destination safely and on time.

Governor Bricker was a tall gracious man who at least 20 times a day would make a little speech from the rear platform of the train at whichever small town we had reached. The local high school band would be there at the station and lead off with a lively rendition of the Stars and Stripes Forever, or some other rousing march. Town officials and other politicos would join the Vice Presidential candidate on the train. Usually there would be a pretty good-sized crowd, generous with applause. The candidate pretty much followed a formula in his speech. When you are making two dozen speeches a day that is understandable. He always said that the high school band of the moment was the best high school band he had seen and heard of all the towns he had visited. Invariably he mentioned what a farmer in Kansas had said to him last week or what a mother of three in Columbus had wanted to know what his position was on this or that. He also mentioned what a mechanic in Michigan thought about the increasing number of foreign made autos coming into the United States or what a small businessman in Denver complained about with respect to taxes. And he always said that in his opinion the town officials of (wherever) were the best in the state of (—).

In an interview with Governor Bricker I handed him a list of questions I had prepared: 1.What high school band was the best he had seen in his campaign? 2. What did a farmer in Kansas say to the candidate? 3. What did that mother of three in Columbus want to know? 4. What group of town officials were the best in what town and state? 5.What was the concern of that mechanic in Michigan? Reading the list, Governor Bricker started laughing and said, "By golly, I'm glad someone has been listening to my speeches." He seemed pleased. Governor Bricker's travels gradually extended eastward to Philadelphia and as Election Day approached he and his train headed westward.

I was instructed by the office to go on up to Albany and cover Governor Dewey's election eve speech and then ride down to New York City on Dewey's special train. Early returns were very encouraging for Dewey but as the evening wore on the tide changed and the Roosevelt-Truman ticket was swept to victory.

After that taste of the big time I was dissatisfied with humdrum reporting so early in 1945 I went in to see Mr. Swanson and told him I would like to have a crack at covering the war in the Pacific. I knew there was an opening there because Phil Heisler had just returned from his assignment with the Navy in that area. The executive editor said he would think it over. In a couple of days he called me in and said I would get the assignment. He also voiced the opinion that the war in the Pacific would go on for another year or two. He said that it would take a few weeks to get me cleared by the Navy and the FBI and that meanwhile he was assigning me to go on the shakedown cruise of a new aircraft carrier, the Antietam, named in memory of a famous Civil War battle in Maryland.

So, for the next three weeks, along with several other reporters, I experienced life on a warship preparing for action in the war against

Japan. As we cruised southward in the Atlantic there were daily flights by the planes of the air group, fighters, bombers and torpedo bombers, who engaged in maneuvers and mock air battles. The carrier's P.R. officer invited the reporters aboard to take a ride in a plane to get an idea of what it was like. I quickly accepted, as did one other in our group. The others declined with thanks.

A CARRIER TAKEOFF

I can attest that a takeoff and a landing on an aircraft carrier can provide you with just about all the thrills you would care to ask for. A torpedo bomber was to be my vehicle. This type of plane normally has a crew of three, the pilot, navigator and gunner. I was to substitute for the gunner who sits in a little cubbyhole under the others in the crew. They warned me that we were going to be shot off the deck by means of a catapult and that I should be prepared for a brief blackout. When I was seated in the cubbyhole I saw there was an iron bar stretched head high in front of me and I was told to grip the bar just as hard as I could. Looking out I could see a deck officer spinning his arm around in circles as fast as he could, telling the pilot to rev the engine to its highest speed and then he threw his fist down toward the deck. Bingo! The next second the plane shot out into the air, the engine groaning loudly. As I had been told I did have a blackout when the blood was driven from my head, but I quickly returned to normal. Then we circled out many miles from the ship and participated in various maneuvers with the other planes.

After a half hour or so we returned to the Antietam, a 26,000-ton vessel and got more of a welcome than we expected. As we came in to land on the deck the landing signal officer waved us off because the plane ahead of us was not yet completely out of the way. So, we had to rejoin the landing circle of planes and when it was our turn we came in and landed without incident.

For the reporters aboard, this was a real pleasure cruise except for the almost constant noise. When the planes weren't taking off or landing, the crews of the 20 and 40-millimeter anti-aircraft guns were sure to be banging away at target practice. Nevertheless, the Navy food was very good and the evenings on deck talking with crewmen were pleasant.

As the Antietam approached the Panama Canal we speculated as to the amount of clearance the ship would have in traversing the canal. It was astonishing to learn that in certain sections of the canal

Our wedding day, September 12, 1939. Florence and I brave a shower of rice.

Reunion in Japan. The author meets up with Axel Malashuk and Bob Cochrane, Sunpapers photographer and reporter respectively.

Tokyo hospitality. The author was seated fifth from left.

As a war correspondent I wore a "C" on my collar and once was mistaken for a chaplain.

the flight deck actually extended over land on both sides. This was possible due to the height of the flight deck.

When we reached Panama City, the Navy P.R person took us out for a tour and among the places we visited was one that, perhaps, should have been omitted. It was called the Villa Amour, a very handsome building of several stories with a bar on the first floor that must have been 40 yards long. Along the bar were stationed dozens of young girls from Brazil and other South or Central American countries. On the upper floors were many bedrooms usefully equipped. Prices for drinks and other things were low, controlled by the Navy. The Villa Amour, we were told, was limited to Navy personnel; open to enlisted men only six days of the week, available to officers only on the seventh day. Our shakedown cruise ended with a Navy flight to Miami and then on to the Patuxent Naval Base in Maryland.

OFF TO WAR

A few days later my journey to the Pacific began at the old, picturesque Mount Royal Railroad Station. Present to see me off was my wife, Florence, of course, and my sister Victoria. Florence hated to see me go but she knew that I always had felt guilty about being safely at home while my brother, Bill, three years my senior, was serving in the infantry in New Guinea and my brother John, two years younger, was a chief petty officer in the Navy somewhere outside the country.

On the four-day journey to the West Coast by train nearly all of my fellow travelers were young soldiers. There was an amusing episode about half way there. I was in uniform as required and on my collar was a gold "C" for correspondent. In the men's room of our car there was a crap game in progress, so I took a turn at throwing the dice. I was about $40 ahead when I needed to throw a four. "Come on, Padre," yelled one of the soldiers, "Make it the hard way." He thought the "C" on my collar designated me as a chaplain. I made the pass and soon dropped out of the game a winner.

War correspondents with the Navy were given an equivalent rank of lieutenant commander, which meant receiving quarters, meals and other perks accorded to officers of that rank. So, when I arrived in San Francisco I was put up at the St. Francis Hotel and told by a P.R. officer that he would get me transportation to Hawaii and on to Guam as soon as possible. Guam was the advanced headquarters for the Navy. A couple of days passed and then I got a hurry up call. "If you can be ready in an hour I can get you a deluxe ride to Hawaii," I was told. When I said I could be ready, I was picked up and driven to the Oakland Airport.

He was certainly right about the deluxe ride. I was put on the official plane of the Secretary of the Navy, James Forrestal. It was a big four engine craft as large as a commercial airliner. It had just been put through a maintenance overhaul and was to pick up Secretary Forrestal in Hawaii and fly him back to Washington. In addition to the plane's crew there were only four or five others on the eight-hour flight to Pearl Harbor.

A couple of leisure days in Hawaii, including a visit to Waikiki Beach, was followed by a 20 hour flight to Guam that required refueling stops at Johnson Island and Kwajalein.

Many months had passed since the Navy and the Marines had retaken Guam from the Japanese. The island was a beehive of activity for it was the headquarters of Admiral Chester Nimitz, Commander in Chief of all Pacific naval forces.

MEETING THE MARINES

On Guam I had the opportunity to meet many officers and men of the 4th Marine Regiment, who not only recaptured Guam but also more recently had retaken Tinian Island.

The Marines were on rest and rehab leave and were waiting, somewhat impatiently, for the arrival of the regiment's expected liquor ration.

While awaiting posting to an aircraft carrier or perhaps some other type of warship, I had to depend on official releases from the Navy or Air Forces operating on Guam for stories to send back to the Sun.

At this time the Air Force B29 bombers were creating havoc in Tokyo and other Japanese cities. The B29's were dropping hundreds of napalm bombs that caused huge fires. The conflagrations were so enormous they sucked up all available oxygen causing many casualties. To do a story about the B29's, I did an interview with General Curtis LeMay who predicted that his planes would bring Japan to its knees. He even announced the names of the cities he was going to bomb and warned that the inhabitants should get out while they could.

The B29's on Guam were taking off from a large airstrip that led to a steep cliff at one end of the island. Along with other reporters I went to the takeoff area where we were permitted to go to the top of a high wooden tower to view the operations. The tower was fairly close to the takeoff point and just off the runway.

We had the opportunity to see the stately bombers being fed onto the main runway and then each would come roaring toward us, rapidly increasing speed. As each plane reached the end of the runway it took off over the ocean and sank down out of sight. Its four engines would be heard groaning mightily to gain altitude. Finally, it would come up in view and wing away toward Japan, many hours away.

Having watched this for a while we were about to come down from the tower when one of the huge planes came racing down the runway with one of its engines shooting flames high into the sky. If its bomb load were touched off the plane, our tower and a large surrounding area would be blown to smithereens.

We hustled down the stairs and saw the plane had been pulled off to one side and the flames extinguished. We were hoping to have a word with the crew but to no avail. A medical officer arrived in a jeep, gave each crewmember a jolt from a bottle of brandy and hustled them away.

About this time I was invited, along with other reporters, to fly to the island of Tinian for a somewhat mysterious mission. When we got there, we were told there was a good story available but it might not pass the censors until some time in the future.

The story? Five large general hospitals were under construction to care for the many casualties that were to be expected when a ground invasion of Japan, planned for the near future, was carried out. Teams of nurses already had arrived to staff the hospitals.

HIROSHIMA BOMBED!

We were still on Tinian when the news of the atomic bombing of Hiroshima burst forth. Orders came to fly back to Guam and await developments. It was only then did we learn that we were within a stone's throw of the bomb before it was loaded aboard the Enola Gay, the plane that carried it to the doomed Japanese city.

For a couple of days all sorts of rumors circulated. The 4th Marine Regiment was embarked on transports and its men were given the honor of being the first American troops to go ashore in Japan to honor the original 4th Marines who had been wiped out at Bataan in the early days of the war.

I had gotten to know many of the young officers of the 4th Marines and it was a pleasure to go along with them to Japan. Most of them had been athletes in college, football, baseball, soccer and lacrosse. They all had war stories to tell. Lieutenant George (Dutch) Proechel liked to recount his harrowing experience the night the Marines fought their way ashore at Guam.

Dutch said he had filled his canteen with brandy instead of water and was feeling no pain ashore even though they were pinned down by Japanese gunfire. At one point in the night he fell into a hole and decided to stay put until daylight. Then he discovered that he had fallen into a Japanese latrine. He was unhurt, he said, but it took a week to get rid of the smell.

On board the transport ship the Marines were distributed to the various decks. The junior officers were stationed four decks down and I went along with them.

Then for more than a week our ship and others slowly proceeded toward Japan. Word spread that the Japanese needed the time to disarm their troops and otherwise prepare for our peaceful landing.

Believe me, those young marines thoroughly enjoyed the cruise. During the day they had little to do but enjoy the breezes on the top deck. But at night, wow! Immediately after evening chow the officers of our deck, far below the brass, would start a well-oiled songfest. Just before embarkation the officers had received the long awaited liquor ration, so now, like magic, many bottles would appear on the tables and the party was on!

SINGING MARINES

It seemed like every man on our deck was a singer or thought he was. Their favorites were Alouette, Blood on the Saddle, As the Caissons Go Rolling Along, and Anchors Aweigh, among many others. This went on every night to the wee hours when even the diehards would give up and retire to the three-tiered bunks. Sometimes it was difficult to get to the top bunk.

Then at last came the day to actually land on Japanese shores. The Marines this day were blessed with a beautiful warm sunny morning. They went over the side of the transport on nets just as they had for combat landings, their landing craft circled until all were in formation and at a signal they raced for the shore, this time at the Yokosuka Naval Base. For the Marines it was a cakewalk, a dress parade. They stepped ashore and immediately set about taking possession of the naval base. The date was August 30, 1945. There were no casualties.

The next day we correspondents took up temporary living quarters on a Navy communications ship, the Ancon, and then went back ashore in a small boat. It should be noted that General MacArthur had issued an order that no one was to go to Tokyo until he issued a general order allowing it. Thus reporters attached to army headquarters had to cool their heels in Yokohama and get their stories from official handouts. Not so for correspondents attached to the Navy. We were free to go anywhere we wanted, write anything we wanted and simply take the copy to the Ancon, where it would be radioed to America without benefit of MacArthur's censorship.

That morning after hitching a ride from Yokosuka to Yokohama, Wilfred Burchett, of the London Daily Express, William McGaffin, of the Chicago Daily News and I visited the Yokohama Office of the Domei news agency where we were greeted by a Japanese who had worked in Washington for five years before the war.

He volunteered to be our guide, so we started for the forbidden territory, Tokyo, on an electric powered train that got us there in less than one hour.

JAPANESE REACTION

But it was in the Yokohama station that we got our first reaction from Japanese civilians and demobilized soldiers. There was friendliness from some and indifference from others.

On the train, which was crowded, there were many curious looks at first. We were obliged to stand only a few minutes when several Japanese in uniform, but unarmed, insisted that we take their seats. We were in uniform also, and like the Japanese, unarmed.

For miles on both sides of the railway line stretched the desolation wrought by firebombs. This entire section had been built up with homes and shops. Now the buildings were rubble with people living in shacks made of rusted metal sheets.

Even in Tokyo the destruction from the firebomb raids was almost unbelievable. Whole acres of built-up areas had been burned to the ground.

We felt a little funny in Tokyo because American troops had not been permitted to enter the city. Any American encountered in Tokyo, and there were a few, were there in defiance of MacArthur's orders.

We made our way toward the Imperial Palace and found in the area a building occupied by Domei news. Ito Hasegawa, who operated Domei's London office for many years before the war, volunteered his services to get us rooms in the Dai itchi Hotel that was built in American style and somehow had managed to avoid destruction.

Each of us was given a bedroom, sitting room and bath on the 8th and top floor. That sounds good but there were drawbacks. The elevators were not running and water connections to the bathrooms were broken. Everytime you went in or out you had to walk the eight flights of stairs and to wash, a maid had to bring up a bucket of water the same way.

It must be said that the manager of the hotel did his best to please. With apologies, he asked us to take our meals in a private dining room rather than in the hotel's main dining hall, saying that it would be the best way to avoid any possibility of unpleasantness on the part of the hotel's other guests, all of them Japanese and quite a few of them soldiers.

By this time it was 4 pm, so we went out for a stroll to kill a couple of hours until dinner would be served. The streets were crowded with Japanese, hundreds of them soldiers in uniform, but unarmed.

The Emperor's Palace, damaged in an air raid some months before, appeared from a distance to be substantially intact. We couldn't approach closely because a company of armed Japanese soldiers was there on guard.

On the way back to the hotel we encountered a bearded white Russian who had been doing propaganda broadcasting for the Japanese for most of the war, a male Tokyo Rose.

When we filed into our private dining room we were greeted by the hotel manager, the head waiter, a couple of serving waiters and a Japanese girl wearing a purple kimono whose sole function during the dinner was to fan us because it was a very warm August evening and, of course, the air conditioning was not working. Our dinner was a pleasant surprise. A salad served with hot bread, a bowl of fish soup, which was followed by a T-bone steak, French-fried potatoes and asparagus. Three quart bottles of beer were brought in and, later, coffee. Subsequently, the Domei manager supplied us with paper, typewriters and desks at which to work. He said that until the Emperor called on the military to lay down their arms, civilians and soldiers alike were resigned to fight to the bitter end.

THE EMPEROR'S DECISION

My biggest story out of Japan, to me more important than my share of the coverage of the Japanese formal surrender on the battleship Missouri, was obtained from the previously mentioned Ito Hasegawa, Foreign Service manager of the Domei News Agency, which, de facto, was part of the Japanese government.

Mr. Hasegawa told me that the Japanese Emperor had decided as early as June 22 to surrender to the Americans, long before the atomic bombs were used and the Russians entered the war. He said the Emperor decided to call it quits after losing all confidence in the leadership of the Japanese army. The Sun carried my story under banner front page headlines on September 4th, two days after the formal surrender, and the Associated Press played it big all over the country, crediting it to me by name as an exclusive report.

Hasegawa and I had become pretty good friends after I obtained for him a large quantity of razor blades he could give to his father. He said he knew he was taking a bit of a risk in telling me the story. He went on to say that while the Japanese navy staked all its remaining strength in defense of Okinawa, the last bastion between the Americans and Japan itself, the army did not. The army wanted to conserve its strength until the homeland was invaded.

The Emperor disagreed with that position and on June 22nd held a secret meeting with certain cabinet ministers and elder statesmen and decided then and there to sue for peace. The decision was kept secret from the people and the army leaders.

Efforts were made to get Russia to mediate but failed and the war dragged on with ever mounting casualties until the Hiroshima and Nagasaki nuclear bombings compelled surrender.

The Sun had three reporters on the Battleship Missouri to cover the surrender ceremonies. They were Robert Cochrane, attached to MacArthur's headquarters; Philip Potter, who had been covering the war in China and your correspondent, attached to the Navy.

My article on the surrender was understandably about the Navy's huge part in bringing about the Japanese defeat. For much of the Pacific war it was all Navy and its marines.

AMERICAN WAR PRISONERS

Two days after the surrender I was riding along a Tokyo street with George Burns, a photographer for Yank Magazine, in an old Japanese car he had liberated when we were hailed by a large group of American prisoners of war who had liberated themselves from a Japanese prison 400 miles from Tokyo.

There were 64 men in the group, emaciated, but happy and in a celebratory mood. "Where the hell are the marines?" was the greeting I got. They were khaki clad and at first we thought they were occupying troops. George Burns remarked it looked like the army had decided to come into Tokyo at last. We screeched to a stop and immediately we were surrounded by the liberated marines. They said we were the first Americans they had seen, other than fellow prisoners, since they were captured. They wanted to know where were the Marines and the Army. I told them the Army was still at Yokohama and that the 4th Marines were based at Yokosuka. "The 4th Marines" they shouted "we are all that's left of the 4th Marines." I explained to them that a new 4th Marine Regiment had been created in honor of the old outfit and had been given the honor of being the first American troops to reach Japanese soil. Just tell us how to get to this Yokosuka and these new 4th Marines will take care of us, they said. Although they were in a hurry to get along, they patiently gave me their names and hometowns so their families could be officially notified that they were alive and well.

Most of my remaining stories from Japan were of a non-serious nature. For example, I was invited to attend a grape gathering festival by a member of the Japanese parliament who was running for reelection. In Baltimore, politicians love their crab feasts and oyster roasts. In Japan it can be a grape gathering but the politics are pretty much the same.

The Diet member, a Mr. Kasai, sent correspondents an invitation that mentioned he had studied at the University of Chicago and Harvard and stated that he wanted to repay the kindness shown to him at both places. The invitation also stated that a special train had been chartered to take us to the grape gathering picnic in the province of Yamanishi prefecture—he called it the Switzerland of Japan.

After proceeding through numerous tunnels through the mountains west of Tokyo the five coach train arrived at the town of Kofu where the passengers could look down into a beautiful valley completely encircled by mountains.

Mr. Kasai and his political cohorts led the party of picnickers up stone steps to the top of an ancient castle. There he delivered a flowery speech, which some cynics said was to show how many American friends he had, thereby helping his reelection campaign.

Following the speech, the picnickers were taken to a pavilion where large supplies of fresh milk were provided. This was a big hit with everyone. Then, in a small fleet of busses, we were driven to a community in the heart of the valley. This place could well qualify as the Shangri-La of Japan. Completely untouched by the war, surrounded by many acres of grapes, apples, corn and other vegetables, its inhabitants seem to be the best fed and happiest in Japan. We sat at bamboo tables and were served a great variety of foods and, of course, grapes. It developed that the picnickers were not to gather grapes but to eat them. Also provided were a great many bottles of grape and apple wines.

FUN IN TOKYO

With each passing day, Tokyo itself became more of a picnic ground for American occupation forces. Literally thousands of American soldiers, sailors and marines swarmed the streets. Many visited the outer grounds of the Imperial Palace where Japanese policemen and American soldiers guarded the gates. In the shade of a gnarled tree, twisted by the winds of centuries, an American soldier sat on the grass sketching the palace, the arched stone bridges over a fish filled moat and a temple with a six-tiered roof. Several Japanese children watched over his shoulder.

Typical of the visitors were jeep-loads of Marines from the 4th Regiment stationed at Yokosuka. With little to do except guard the Naval Base, the 4th frequently made the forty mile round trip for recreation. One afternoon a group of these Marines spied two Japanese pulling rickshaws on one of the main downtown streets. The Marines began dickering for the use of the two-wheeled, hand drawn vehicles and waved the two Japanese to seats on the curb. Then they began staging races with the rickshaws, one Marine a passenger in each and one Marine as a puller. With loud whoops from the participants, the rickshaws careened up and down the streets at perilous speeds, watched with consternation by hundreds of Japanese. When all were well nigh exhausted, they paid off the rickshaw owners with cigarettes, then headed back to Yokosuka.

One of the strangest stories I encountered resulted from a visit to my friends in the 4th Marines. I was invited to go for an exploratory jeep trip with Lieut. Robert Cutter and previously mentioned Lieut. Dutch Proechel. We loaded up with food and some beer and went to see what we could see.

We were riding through the mountains and the jeep was having a little difficulty negotiating the steep, winding little road when, to our surprise, we saw sitting on a roadside bench two pretty and nicely dressed girls who obviously were Europeans. With them was a serious looking bespectacled man. Lieut. Cutter stopped the jeep and we got another surprise when we learned that all three spoke English.

THE LOST COLONY

Somehow it seemed too fantastic to be true to find in this rugged spot, amid towering, pine crested bluffs, deep gorges and tumbling waterfalls, these rosy-cheeked girls and their escort, who turned out to be a chemist, sitting there miles from any habitation and seemingly unconcerned about it.

We had stumbled, we learned, onto a "lost colony" of some 300 German men, women and children leading a fairy-tale life in and near the little village of Myanoshita high in the mountains of Honshu. Cut off from their homeland, these former sailors, marines and experts in the chemical industry were facing the future without much hope. Looked down upon by the Japanese, who had become openly hostile since Germany had been defeated, these Germans were subsisting on meager stocks of food provided by the Nazi government before the 3rd Reich collapsed. Their homes, built with their own hands in these precipitous cliffs after they had been forced to flee from bomb-torn Tokyo and Yokohama, were little more than shacks.

The girls we encountered, Else Heun, 17, and her sister, Tilde, 21, said they had started out in a vain quest for some fresh vegetables and had walked several miles to a neighboring village. Empty handed, they and their escort, Heinrich Bahrt, had started the long, uphill walk to the German community and were resting in the hope that some form of transportation might come along. They said the Japanese occasionally operated an ancient bus along the mountain road. Lieut. Cutter gave the trio a little surprise when he began conversing in German which he had learned while studying medicine in Germany in 1938. Lieut. Proechel, who used to play professional baseball and coached a high school team, passed around cigarettes and off we started up the mountain.

It was the first time the Germans had ever seen a jeep and they said the cigarettes were the first real smoke they had had in several years. Japanese cigarettes, they said, were made of some kind of grass, definitely not tobacco. A half hour ride brought us to the frame buildings of the colony and we were invited into the largest building which they used as a bakery. They sat us down in homemade chairs at a homemade table and there we spent a most unusual afternoon and evening. The Germans produced a bottle of Japanese wine and sandwiches made with fresh baked bread. Not to be outdone, Lieut. Cutter went out to the jeep and came back with six large bottles of Japanese beer and the food we had brought for the trip. There followed a singing session in which it appeared that the entire colony participated. It lasted for hours.

It was very late at night when we arrived back at Yokosuka after a perilous drive through heavy rains. Before leaving the "lost colony," Lieut. Cutter promised its occupants that he would alert American and German authorities of their plight.

My remaining weeks in Japan were uneventful and I was delighted when the office told me that I should return home as soon as I could arrange for transportation.

HOMEWARD BOUND

Eventually, I was able to get on a plane to Guam. After several days there I was lucky enough to get aboard the hospital ship Tranquility which was taking about 800 injured men to San Francisco.

Lo and behold, one of the first persons I met on the Tranquility was my closest neighbor in the Northwood Apartments in Baltimore, Naval Commander James Bunn, Chief Radiologist on the hospital ship. The doors to our second floor apartments were less than six feet apart and our wives were close friends.

Commander Bunn was graduated from the University of Maryland Medical School and was in charge of the x-ray department on the Tranquility. In fact, there was a strong Maryland contingent on the hospital ship. The senior officer, Capt. Bart Hogan and the Chief Urologist, Commander Hugh Warren, were both from Annapolis.

My wife, Florence, her parents, Mr. and Mrs. Herman Reich, and my 3 year old son, Tom, Jr., were at the railroad station in Baltimore to greet me as I completed the transcontinental train trip home.

After a few weeks vacation, I was assigned to cover the newly formed United Nations organization then housed in a building at Hunter College in New York City. For the next six months I covered the U.N. at Hunter College and then at their new home in Flushing Meadows. Five days a week I lived at the famed Algonquin Hotel, where the Sun had a year round lease on a suite of rooms. Then on Friday night after filing the day's story to the paper, I would take the train home to Baltimore. On Sunday night I would take the 10 P.M. train for New York to get ready for the coming week. Coverage at the U.N. then, as now, consisted mostly of reporting on speeches often in foreign languages translated by official linguists. Exciting events were few and far between. So it was a relief to me and my family when I was reassigned to Baltimore.

But that didn't mean that I was going to be able to stay at home. As a "field correspondent" I was sent out to cover the unveiling of the first main computer at the University of Pennsylvania, to do a series of articles on bootlegging in Kansas and Tennessee and to cover combined military maneuvers in Puerto Rico to mention just a few of the many assignments around the country.

OFF TO PUERTO RICO

The assignment to cover the Navy-Marine maneuvers in Puerto Rico was noteworthy, at least to me, because it involved my participation in a demonstration of air-sea rescue work.

Officers of a Navy blimp taking part in the exercises were anxious to get some publicity because they were hearing rumors that the blimp service might be discontinued.

Lieut. M.M. Hill, the blimp commander, asked for advice. I suggested they could show the usefulness of blimps in picking up sick or wounded men from ships at sea or deliver something or someone to a ship, for example a doctor or a new ship captain.

They latched on to the latter suggestion and asked would I volunteer to be the someone to be delivered from the blimp to a ship, arguing that since a reporter would be involved it would be more likely that the admiral in command of the maneuvers would give his approval.

Since I had brought the whole thing up it was with some trepidation that I agreed to do it if the admiral approved. He did and that was that. The flight, which had as its culmination the transfer of the passenger to the deck of the Salerno Bay, an escort carrier anchored at sea, began about 8 A.M. from San Juan when the blimp headed for the Navy task force at sea.

As the blimp neared the ships, hundreds of faces were turned upward as we circled around the carrier. Meanwhile, the passenger was given a cup of coffee to steady his nerves, equipped with a life jacket and told to sit in the canvas "basket" from which I would be delivered. The basket was about 3 feet in diameter, with four ropes running from the edges to join a thicker main rope just above the head of the basket occupant. There were two leg slits in the canvas seat but it was felt that in an emergency their use might prevent a quick exit if needed. So, the passenger was advised to sit in the center of the canvas, dangle his legs over the side and hold firmly to two of the ropes with each hand.

Then when we were about 1,000 feet above the ocean we were set to perform the "drop." Sitting on, not in the canvas seat, I was lifted from the deck of the blimp's gondola and swung through a port out into the air. The crewmen paid out 30 or 40 feet of rope that they had snubbed around a pole. I actually did experience a drop and when it was checked I spun around like a top. I tightened my grip on the ropes and hung on for dear life. Flying lower, the blimp approached the aircraft carrier. I could hear a voice on the ship's loudspeaker explaining what the demonstration was about. Skillfully maneuvering over the ship, the blimp's crew landed me on the carrier's deck without a hitch and we received a "well done" broadcast by Rear Admiral R.O. Whitehead, Commander of Carrier Division 14. I did an article on the event which was published with pictures in the Sun's rotogravure Sunday magazine. Copies were sent to the Navy's public relations division. The Navy wrote a thank you note of appreciation.

My first appearance on television occurred when shortly after the war I was assigned to interview Major James P. Devereaux, the hero of Wake Island. He was the commander of a small detachment of Marines on Wake Island, then a refueling station for American naval vessels. Immediately after the attack on Pearl Harbor, a large force of Japanese warships and soldiers attacked Wake Island.

Major Devereaux and the Marines put up a valiant fight against an enemy force of overwhelming strength. At the height of the battle the Navy put out a report that Devereaux had defiantly challenged, "Send us more Japs." In the interview, the Major said, "That was pure hokum, we had more Japs than we could handle." He spent years in Japan as a prisoner of war.

I was rounding out 16 years at the Sun in the spring of 1949 and for some time had become increasingly bored with newspaper work.

ANOTHER LIFE CHANGE

Then, out of the blue, there occurred an incident that again completely changed my life.

I was walking past the City Hall about noon, one day, when Mayor Tommy D'Alesandro and Neil McCardell, City Comptroller, came out. They were going to lunch and the Mayor invited me to join them. I had known him since his days in the City Council.

We went to a nearby restaurant known as "10 Downing Street," because it was the favorite hangout of half the politicians in town. Neil McCardell went table hopping shaking hands with political cronies while the Mayor and I sat down and ordered. While awaiting for our

Making it official, Tom O'Donnell signs on as Baltimore's Publc Relations Director. Mayor D'Alesandro, observes, May 1949.

The mayor and a half dozen news reporters off on a junket to the Miles River regatta.

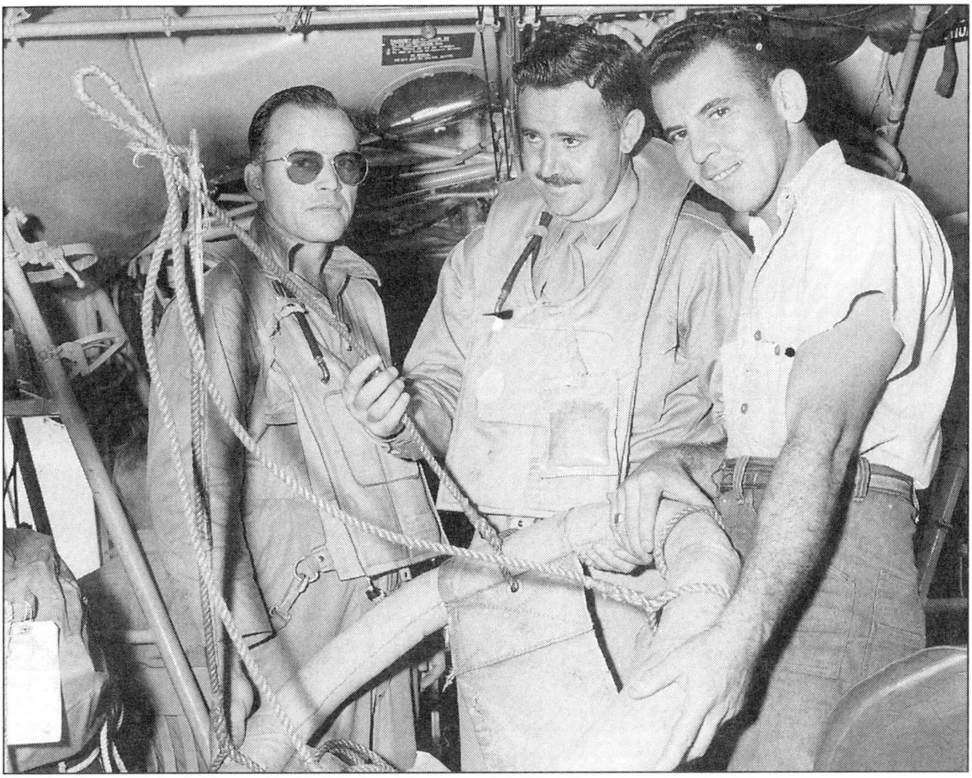

Author inspects the "seat" in which he will be lowered from a blimp to the deck of a ship at sea.

Approaching target ship. All is well so far.

Almost there as those on deck reach for trailing rope.

Mission accomplished as author is greeted by Rear Admiral R. F. Whitehead.

food, the Mayor remarked that he badly needed somebody to help him with speeches and publicity and could I recommend somebody for the job. I thought for a minute and then I said, "How about me?" He looked surprised and said would you consider something like that. I told him yes, I would consider it. Then he asked what I was making at the Sun and I gave him a figure that was a couple of thousand more than I was getting. Well, he said, I could go three or four thousand more than that to start with. You've got a deal, I told him, and we shook hands on it. The whole thing was done by the time McCardell got back to the table.

The Mayor wanted to announce it right away, but I told him that I felt obliged to give the newspaper three weeks notice. He agreed to that, but couldn't resist telling the City Hall reporters that he was going to hire a municipal public relations director, for that was the title I was to have, although the name of the appointee was to remain secret for the present.

I turned in a written resignation and received a written reply from the managing editor stating that since I was entitled to three weeks vacation, I was free to leave at will.

Moving into the City Hall seemed to give me a new lease on life. I was now 38 years old, married for 10 years, and my son Tom, Jr., was going on 8. Florence never once questioned my decision to leave a relatively safe job and sail into uncharted waters.

In my new position I was answerable to no one but the mayor and we got along famously, as it turned out. He trusted my judgment and he received absolute loyalty and respect in return.

On my first day in office, the Mayor and I had a meeting with the City Hall newsmen and other reporters and I told them I would cooperate with them in every way possible.

This wasn't too difficult because I knew them all anyway and was on friendliest terms with them.

In those first days I did a lot of thinking about how I could be useful to the mayor and to the people of Baltimore.

The Mayor was not given to long formal speeches at luncheons, banquets and other civic functions so my obligation with respect to providing speech material was limited to a few paragraphs containing what he described as "the meat in the coconut." Then he would render one of his off the cuff orations for which he was famous.

When Mayor D'Alesandro was elected to the first of his three terms in 1947 he fell heir to a city in dire need of rehabilitation.

Of necessity during World War II, city maintenance and improvements were out the window. Most of the streets were filled with ruts, schools were run down, street lighting was poor, garbage collections were irregular and things generally were a mess.

REPORTING IMPROVEMENTS

Mr. D'Alesandro launched a vast program of improvements, but the people of Baltimore had heard little or nothing about the progress being made. It was my job to get the facts together and inform the public about what was happening and what to look for in the future. Almost daily we had written statements to distribute to the press but the reporters also had easy access to the Mayor when in his office and not out breaking ground for some new city project. My own office was right next to the Mayor's small private office which adjoined the large, ornate official office used for receptions, ordinance signings and the like.

Among my duties was dealing with various civic organizations such as the Citizens' Planning and Housing Association, the Women's Civic League and the Association of Commerce, a city-wide organization of business executives.

At the end of his first year in office Mayor D'Alesandro had released reports prepared by the various municipal departments but they were technical and dry as dust and got very little press notice.

It was at the end of the Mayor's second year as chief executive that I came into the picture. It was my aim to prepare for public consumption a report in magazine style, loaded with pictures, architects' renderings and copy presented in readable form that would attract the attention of business and civic organizations as well as the newspapers and radio stations.

This first of a number of publications was a 48 page report containing photos of the Mayor, flanked by civic leaders, breaking ground for 11 major projects including new schools, hospital buildings, health centers, recreation facilities and the city's first off street parking project. There were depictions of the harbor cleanup, newly paved streets, and of other improvements to come.

In center fold fashion, there were head photographs of the 20 City Councilmen. This was followed by a large photo of the President of the City Council and an account of his activities.

Similarly, there were photos and brief statements by the City Comptroller, the City Solicitor and the Director of Public Works, all

Typical scene at one of the scores of ground breakings for the greatest program of public improvements in Baltimore history.

Reporting on first 10 years of the D'Alesandro administration, a brochure depicts some of the 68 major improvement projects schools, health building, stadium, etc.

four of whom, with the Mayor, made up the Board of Estimates, the top administrative body of the city.

The report attracted a good deal of notice and, in general, was widely approved by business and civic leaders.

In subsequent years, there were similar reports and in 1957, there was a report, in brochure form, entitled Progress in Baltimore, 1947 – 1957.

The brochure contained 68 photos of completed capital projects including 26 large new schools; the new Memorial Stadium, which made it possible to bring big league baseball back to Baltimore; Friendship International Airport, now called Baltimore Washington Airport; the Sam Smith Waterfront Park, which led to the Inner Harbor development; numerous new recreation centers, health facilities; new markets; firehouses; branch libraries and much more

Engineers and others commented that the improvements made represented a half century of progress in the ordinary course of events.

Meanwhile, the city's antiquated gas lamp lighting system was completely replaced with electric lights.

Baltimore became the first large city in the world to add fluorine to its drinking water, benefiting hundreds of thousands of children in the city and adjacent counties that receive city water, reducing tooth cavities tremendously.

In a brief text accompanying the pictorial decade report, the Mayor noted that the tax rate in 1957 was $2.88 as compared with $2.96 when he took office in 1947. Additionally he pointed out that the independent Efficiency and Economy Commission reported Baltimore's debt ratio to its taxable basis was less in 1957 than in 1947.

Also built in the D'Alesandro years was the Civic Center, now known as the Baltimore Arena. I was appointed to the Civic Center Commission for 2 terms. As mentioned earlier, the chairman of the Commission was Charles P. McCormack

Altogether, my first year as Director of Public Relations was an extremely busy one. As previously mentioned, one of my first projects on the job was to bring a big league professional golf tournament to Baltimore. I discussed the idea with the mayor and he was all for it. He said follow up on it and keep me posted. I wrote to my brother John who was the golf professional at a Virginia country club and a member of the PGA, and asked for his advice on how to proceed. He told me to get in touch with Tom Crane, General Counsel to the PGA and my brother also gave me a lot of advice on tournament preparation. So I wrote to Mr. Crane and told him that the Mayor of Baltimore was interested in bringing a PGA event to this city. Crane wrote back the schedule of tournaments for 1950, was completely filled, but that he would keep us in mind for the future. A few weeks later Crane telephoned to say that they had received a cancellation for a date in September and asked whether we would be interested in hosting a tournament for that time period.

PGA TOURNEY FOR BALTIMORE

We set the wheels in motion at once. Mr. Crane was informed that we were greatly interested and he was requested to let us know what the PGA required of us. Meanwhile the Mayor made a public announcement that the city was seeking a PGA tournament and that he had appointed me as general chairman of the Mayor's Committee. To enlist other members of the committee was left up to me. Crane wrote back that the contract he had enclosed provided that there had to be a purse of $35,000 guaranteed by a financial sponsor and that it should be signed and returned as soon as possible.

Winners of PGA tournaments in those days were getting $3,500 and a trophy. Now they get from half a million up to a million dollars. I landed a financial sponsor on my first try. After telephoning the advertising department of the Gunther Brewing Company for an appointment, I went out to their plant and in less than an hour sold the heads of their advertising and legal departments and got the necessary signatures to the contract. Now the Mayor was able to announce that the tournament was a reality. He immediately wrote to the Board of Recreation and Parks requesting use of the Mount Pleasant golf course for the tourney. The Park Board quickly approved the request and directed Charles (Gus) Hook, head of the Parks Department to get the Mount Pleasant course in the best condition possible. Gus, a regular golfer himself, went all out to comply.

The Mount Pleasant course was known as one of the best public courses in the country and some years before had hosted the National Public Links Championship.

With the publicity given to the coming tournament both the Mount Pleasant men's and women's golf associations volunteered to act as marshals, scorers and in other capacities which made the filling out of the Mayor's Committee easy.

We tried all sorts of things to promote the tournament. Downtown

The author's family supporters at one of the Eastern Open tourneys. From left, niece Michelle, Sister Victoria, wife Florence, son Francis, niece Pat and son Tom, Jr.

Mayor roots for the newly arrived big league Orioles in 1954. man on far right was one of the owners, Bill Callahan, author in middle.

department stores, upon request, put together window displays featuring star professional golfers. The main downtown library did the same and the then famous Miller Brothers restaurant provided promotional matchbooks on all their tables.

Local television stations put on shows featuring Baltimore golf professionals and the pros at all the golf courses in and near the city put promotional placards in their shops and sold tickets.

The Baltimore Sun helped a great deal and provided the very important service of overseeing the sale of tickets and the funds received for these.

As the tournament time approached there was one big headache developing. The Mount Pleasant course then did not have a watering system as it does now and because of a dry summer the course, except for the putting greens, was drying up.

Baltimore's director of Public Works, George Carter, saved the day. He ordered the city's fleet of sprinkler trucks be diverted to the golf course and soon they were being driven up and down the fairways.

The week before our tournament the National Open was being held at the famous Merion Cricket Club in Philadelphia. My brother John was playing in it, so I had two reasons to go up to Merion. The other reason was that it afforded me the opportunity to study how a big tournament was conducted. The tournament at Merion resulting in a tie involving Ben Hogan, one of the all-time great players and Lloyd Mangrum, a dashing figure sometimes called the "Riverboat Gambler," that called for a 36 hole playoff, won by Hogan. Mangrum fared better at our tourney, winning it with a four round score of 279, nine under par.

Our tournament was named the Eastern Open by me in an effort to give it a little more distinction and it was a huge success. The Baltimore Sun, my former employer, was generous in an editorial the day after the event, praising me by name, and expressing the hope that the tournament be made a permanent annual fixture. That hope was fulfilled. The tourney was run by me for the next nine years and had most of the big names in golf, including Sam Snead and Arnold Palmer, as winners. The Mayor was there annually to award the winner the D'Alesandro trophy and the prize money. For three of those years the Sun was the financial sponsor of the tourneys.

Brimming over with energy and enthusiasm, Mayor D'Alesandro played an essential role in bringing big league baseball back to Baltimore and was a leader in getting the football team that became the Baltimore Colts. Tom Biddison, the city solicitor, and I were with the Mayor when he went to Washington to meet with Bill Veeck, the owner of the St. Louis Browns big league baseball team. Veeck was looking for a city to which he could move the team because of poor fan support in St. Louis. When the Mayor assured Veeck that he would give all out support to plans for moving the team, Veeck asked what Baltimore law firm he should hire for the legal proceedings. The Mayor said Veeck didn't need to hire any local law firm. If there are any legal problems that have to be solved, he continued, Tom Biddison here will handle the problem for you.

With respect to the future Baltimore Colts, the prospective local owners wanted some assurance that Baltimoreans would support the Texas team they were thinking about buying and moving here. As a test, an exhibition game was scheduled here and the fan turnout was very good. With a personal letter to his legion of friends the mayor single handedly sold $35,000 worth of tickets for the game. As a result the team was brought to Baltimore.

THE CIVIC CENTER

Later on, efforts to build a sports arena to house hoped for professional basketball and hockey teams were blocked for many months by fierce debates over possible sites.

The D'Alesandro administration favored a location on the shore of the Druid Hill Park lake-reservoir, arguing the building and its surroundings could be made to "rival the Taj Mahal" for beauty.

The opponents wanted the building in the downtown area. Department store owners argued that it would bring business to downtown. At the same time, the big store owners were building large branch stores in suburban areas, thus taking business out of the downtown areas. Other opponents argued against the use of any park area for the building and still others wanted to build it right on the waterfront, the site that is now the famous Inner Harbor development.

The Mayor had one of his adherents introduce an ordinance in the City Council to authorize the use of the Druid Hill Park site. A hearing on the ordinance was scheduled and the three Baltimore television stations made an arrangement to carry the hearing live, as they do Congressional hearings on legislation today. For Baltimore, this was a first.

The Mayor designated me to represent the administration, knowing of my experience on television. I was the opening witness and

Mayor welcomes prize winning contestant at 1950 Eastern open.

Mayor D'Alesandro awards trophy to a young Arnold Palmer, winner of the 1956 Eastern Open golf tournament.

Tournament director and his brother, home pro John O'Donnell, inspect Mount Pleasant course before a tournament.

Author and wife, Florence, at one of the Eastern Open Tourneys.

Mayor D'Alesandro and Dr. Cary Middlecoff, winner of 1951 Eastern Open.

Mayor D'Alesandro signs autographs for young fans at golf tourney.

Mayor D'Alesandro talks things over with John O'Donnell, home pro for Eastern Open at Mount Pleasant.

Mayor D'Alesandro congratulates local professional Charley Bassler, an Eastern Open prize winner.

Swearing in members of Civic Center commission. Third from left, Charles P. McCormick, who employed the youthful Tommy D'Alesandro, at spice factory, author at far right end.

The Mayor with "Terrible Tommy" Bolt, winner of 1957 Tourney.

Ready for the new Orioles, from left, Jack Dunn, 3rd, owner of the minor league Orioles; Mr. and Mrs. Clarence Miles, part owners of big league Orioles, the author and Mayor and Mrs. Nancy D'Alesandro.

spoke extemporaneously for 45 minutes outlining the need for the Civic Center, the availability of the park site, which would save a great deal of money and the possibilities for in-house parking without "desecrating" the park.

After this I answered questions fired at me by City Council members opposed to the ordinance. Chief among them was a young William Donald Schaeffer, who later was to become Mayor, Governor and State Comptroller.

During all this, the Mayor, Tom Biddison and other city officials were in the Mayor's private office watching the TV. When I concluded my part in the hearing Mayor D'Alesandro pronounced my presentation as "superb," but said he was afraid I might lose my temper over Schaeffer's badgering. Opponents of the ordinance put up strong arguments against it but the Council approved the measure within an hour after the hearing was concluded. That was not the end of the matter, however, the Board of Recreation and Parks voted against the plan and it and other opponents brought suit in opposition in Circuit Court.

The Court struck down the ordinance on the ground that the Park Board had the power under the City Charter to block it. The Mayor decided not to appeal the court's decision. Therefore, the Civic Center (Baltimore Arena) stands today downtown but the department stores are gone.

My television experience mostly came about through the weekly TV show, "Your City Government."

Not long after I went to work at the City Hall I made a telephone call to Station WBAL-TV and asked to speak to their public relations officer.

In those early years of television, the stations seemed much more aware of their obligation, under law, to provide public service programs than, perhaps, they are today.

When I outlined what I had in mind and asked if the station would provide the city with airtime, the station executive said he liked the idea and would get me an answer without delay. A day or so later I received a call that the city would have 15 minutes at its disposal every Tuesday night at 7 o'clock, a very good time. WBAL gave us some good promotional publicity and the program was launched with Mayor D'Alesandro and Paul Holland, then city Director of Public Works, as the program's first guests. The Mayor insisted that he have a little something on paper that he could read when I introduced him, which was simply a matter of form because his was the best known face in town. Paul Holland also made a little prepared talk and then there was still ten minutes time remaining. That can seem like a long time on television where one minute "sound bites" are in vogue these days. The Mayor and Holland looked a little panicky for a moment but both relaxed when I casually began asking them questions about the events of the day and soon they were both gabbing away about their activities and enjoying it thoroughly.

During the following year every city official of importance, and many not so important, appeared on the program and had their " 15 minutes of celebrity" explaining what their duties were and how they performed them. Even the ladies who worked in the Mayor's office had their 15 minutes of fame on the show and they got a real kick out of it.

At the end of the year I asked the station to give us a half hour so that everyone who had appeared on the show could participate in a little celebration. This was done and the studio was crowded with more than a hundred men and women to be reintroduced and take a bow. As the time for the Mayor's reelection campaign of 1951 was coming up it was felt that to avoid charges of partisanship the program was discontinued.

SCHOOL CHILDREN AT CITY HALL

Among the nicest activities that went on in the City Hall were visits by classes of school children from both public and private schools. The children of elementary and high school age would visit the mayor's office and if he happened to be in they would receive a welcoming handshake from him. Then they would go upstairs for a visit to the City Council chamber and a possible meeting with the President of the City Council.

It occurred to me that with the concurrence of the Mayor, the Council, the Women's Civic League and school officials, both public and private, I could create a pamphlet, "Your City Government" for distribution to the school children and others visiting City Hall. Approval gained, I went ahead with the pamphlet. Its front cover had in bold type, "Your City Government," and beneath the heading was a very good photograph of Baltimore's stately City Hall. The first inside page contained a foreword explaining that the city was governed by the Mayor–City Council form of government, that the Mayor and the President of the City Council are elected on a citywide basis for 4 year

Author as an instructor, with University of Baltimore's Dean James. Subject: Governmental Public Relations

"Your City Government" was subject of weekly TV program. From right: Mayor D'Alesandro, Paul Holland, a top city official, and author on inaugural program.

terms; that members of the City Council were elected from councilmanic districts, also for 4 year terms and that local laws enacted by them could not exceed in scope the authority granted by the City Charter, which was comparable in local matters with the U.S. Constitution in national legislation. The pamphlet also included many bits of information about the city government. Thousands of copies of the pamphlet were distributed over the years.

Working for the Mayor was really a great source of satisfaction. If you went to him with what you considered to be a good idea he gave you a complete hearing and more often than not he gave you a go ahead signal. Not only that, he was enthusiastic, cheerful, outgoing, friendly and had a great sense of humor. His energy was legend. He would work all day and then continue far into the evening. Early in our association he established a routine of telephoning me at home every night shortly after 9 pm. At that time, each evening he would be in his chauffeur driven car outside the Baltimore Sun building at Charles and Baltimore Streets to get a copy of the Sun's early edition. He would quickly scan the editorial page and the local news to see if there was anything about him or the City Government. Then he would phone me. If there was anything that required a statement from him we would jointly prepare it right there on the telephone.

The Mayor's campaign for a second term, in 1951, turned out to be a picnic. I expected to be roundly criticized for actively participating in the campaign, but it didn't happen. My duties included placement of advertising, production of live television shows and often I was called on to write speeches for adherents who appeared on the shows.

POLITICAL ADS

For the newspapers I created for placement in the Sun a 12-page rotogravure section closely resembling their own Sunday roto magazine. When I took the layout to the Sun they hemmed and hawed, but finally agreed to carry it in the edition on the Sunday before the election. The Sun said the cost would be $15,000 and that this must be paid in advance. Members of the Campaign Committee thought the cost was high but they liked the idea so they came up with the money.

Heading the front page of the Sunday insert was the headline in very large type "The D'Alesandro-McCardell Report". Below that was a big picture of the Mayor breaking ground at a construction site. He was flanked by a crowd of men and women, all laughing at some joke he had made. Below the picture was a banner reading "A Quarter

Century of Progress in Four Years." Filling our the bottom fourth of the page were photos of the Mayor, Neil McCardell, up for re-election as Comptroller, and a new comer on the ticket, Arthur B. Price, running for President of the City Council. More about him later.

On succeeding pages were family photos followed by scads of pictures of new schools, paving projects, health and recreation facilities, etc. Everybody in the campaign loved the roto section. Baltimore politics had never seen anything like it before.

Elsewhere, however, there were a couple of dissenters. When Paul Patterson, the headman at the Sun, returned from traveling in Europe he was reported as saying that if he had been on the scene he would not have allowed its publication. The other complainant was the advertising department of the Baltimore News Post. It had learned by the grapevine about the rotogravure long before it was published and wanted to know what it was going to get. I told the Mayor about the News Post complaint and that they ought to get four or five full page ads to sort of balance the account. Mr. D'Alesandro agreed and got the campaign to provide the funds.

Our campaign was being waged on two fronts, against the democratic candidate, Charles G. Griebel, a businessman, and Joseph L. Carter, the Republican Candidate who had no strong primary opponent.

The Republican forces were spreading rumors that the Mayor had obtained unusually low assessment tax rates on his home. To refute the charge, we got the facts and ran a full page News Post ad showing pictures of Carter's Guilford home and the Mayor's house in Little Italy, overlooking a restaurant. Carter's total assessment was $14,100 and the Mayor's was $14,280. The land was assessed at $1.80 per square foot for the Mayor and only 35 cents for Carter. There was no more talk about assessments after that.

The other News Post ads dealt with "What do the newspapers think of D'Alesandro," which featured a nice selection of news articles and an editorial favorable about the Mayor. Another, "What the Citizens of Baltimore Think about their Mayor" highlighted favorable letters to the Mayor, one of which was from a Baptist minister in South Baltimore who wrote, "Every day I thank God for Mayor D'Alesandro." The Mayor romped to an easy win over Griebel in the primary and Carter in the general election. He celebrated by taking a group of friends, including news reporters, to the Homestead resort hotel where we spent 10 days playing golf, tennis, skeet shooting and gorging on the resort's famous food.

Mayor D'Alesandro celebrates election victory at TV station WMAR. Holding the microphone is the late Dave Stickle.

Mayor D'Alesandro and his office staff, early 1950's.

Celebrating 1951 victory at Homestead Hotel. Standing by carriage, the late Anselm Sodaro then State's Attorney, later chief judge of the Baltimore Bench.

But if the Mayor's high spirits usually prevailed there began episodes of depression that were debilitating to a greater or lesser degree. Recovering from one of these early in 1952 and following his doctor's recommendation, the Mayor decided to take a cruise and he asked that I go along with him.

We embarked from New York on February 9, 1952 and the Mayor's spirits seemed to rise almost immediately.

He wasn't a bit daunted when he received a wireless message from his wife Nancy that rumors were being spread around Baltimore that he was dying.

To dispel the rumors, the Mayor and I went to the ship's gymnasium with the ship's photographer and had pictures of the Mayor and me made sparring in a boxing mode and other photographs showing him skipping rope and riding an exercise bike. We dispatched these photographs via air mail to Baltimore newspapers as soon as the ship arrived at San Juan, Puerto Rico, the first stop on a 16-day cruise that also included visits to ports in the Dominican Republic, Venezuela, Curacao, Jamaica and Havana. Our cruise ship was the Italia, of the Home Lines, noted for delicious food, and fine entertainment.

As soon as the ship arrived in San Juan we were greeted by an official representing the mayor of San Juan, Felisa Rincon De Gautier, inviting the Mayor to a reception in his honor. A grand dame of regal appearance, Alcaldessa De Gautier had been chief executive of San Juan for more than two decades and was beloved by her constituents. Her hospitality matched her great dignity. She treated the Mayor like visiting royalty and took him for a tour of the city and got us back to the ship in time for dinner and "all aboard."

The rest of the cruise was very interesting and healthful for the Mayor. He was entertained as a visiting celebrity in Havana. This was before the advent of Fidel Castro.

FOR BETTER TEETH

In my opinion the highlight during my tenure at City Hall was the inauguration of a project that perhaps had a more good and lasting effect on the people of Baltimore and the surrounding counties than any other carried out by Mayor D'Alesandro. But, there, I may be prejudiced.

It all started when I read some reports published by the United States Public Health Service. They noted that studies showed special benefits were enjoyed by people who lived in communities where the drinking water naturally contained fluorine. These people, it was reported, had better and stronger teeth than was the norm elsewhere and they had fewer cavities by far. The Public Health Service strongly recommended that American cities should make use of fluorine in their water supply. I took this information to the Mayor and suggested he might want to look at it. He became interested immediately and got in touch with Health Commissioner Huntington Williams and said he wanted to fluorinate Baltimore's drinking water.

The Health Commissioner suggested that a study should be made as to the benefits but the Mayor replied that the Federal government's studies were good enough for him. So, an ordinance was introduced in the City council authorizing the Bureau of Water Supply to add the recommended amount of fluorine to the water passing through the municipal filtration plant.

Political opponents of the Mayor put up a fight against the measure alleging that it would endanger the health of all Baltimoreans and the people living in the nearby counties that obtain their drinking water from the city.

The ordinance was passed and approved by the Mayor and in a few weeks the new service was begun. In the ensuing half century hundreds of thousands of children living in or near Baltimore have had better and stronger teeth than those who preceded them.

Surveys by dental authorities have revealed that cavities experienced by children have been reduced dramatically because of fluorination and without side effects.

NEW TRAFFIC CZAR

Another dramatic change in Baltimore was brought about through a story in the Baltimore Sun written by the late Edgar Jones, who was a Sun editorial writer for many years.

It seems that Mr. Jones was in Denver, Colorado, on vacation, where he learned of extraordinary improvement in the traffic situation of that city by a traffic engineer named Henry Barnes.

When this information was relayed to the Mayor, with his usual prompt reaction to anything that might mean an improvement for Baltimore, he got in touch with the Mayor of Denver, and asked whether he could borrow Henry for a few weeks to make a traffic survey of Baltimore and submit recommendations.

The arrival of Mr. Barnes brought a turnout of newspaper, television and radio reporters who accompanied the traffic engineer on his

To refute political rumors that he was "dying" while on a cruise, Mayor D'Alesandro spars with author in ship's gym.

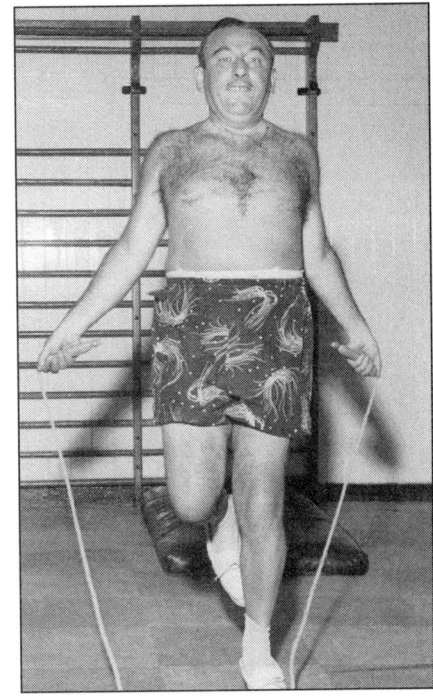

The Mayor tries his hand at jumping rope.

The Mayor's photos of workouts in the cruise ship's gym were airmailed to Baltimore's newspapers from San Juan, Puerto Rico, the first stop on the cruise.

Mayor D'Alesandro was warmly greeted by Madame Felisa Rincon DeGautier, the Mayor of San Juan and treated royally during his brief stay.

Reception at City Hall, San Juan, Puerto Rico. Seated second from right, Mayor DeGautier.

city-wide survey over a period of weeks.

Mr. Barnes returned to Denver and after about a month the report on his survey arrived. It was devastating. He lambasted city officials for permitting traffic snarls to occur and spared no one in his criticism. Then he outlined in detail the many things that should be done, must be done, to cure the problems.

The upshot of it was Mr. Barnes was hired to come to Baltimore as traffic czar at a salary larger than the Mayor's own, and in a few years wrought many changes for the better in the city's traffic patterns. He did so well, in fact, he was hired away from Baltimore by, you might know, the Big Apple, New York City.

CENSORSHIP!

It seemed at times that we were always getting into some controversy at the City Hall. This time it involved a telephone call to me from a prominent member of the Women's Civic League who asked if I was aware of a picture called "In a room" on display at the Municipal Museum on Holliday Street.

When I told her that I had not been in the museum for some time she said you better go over there and take a look at it. I did so and I understood her concern for it depicted naked figures on a bed and was not the sort of fare suitable for the classes of school children who visited the museum on their field trips to nearby City Hall. I went right to the Mayor and told him about the telephone call and what I had seen.

He immediately called Tom Biddison, the City Attorney, and the three of us went over and viewed the picture. The Mayor asked Biddison for his opinion and the attorney said, "Let's get the museum director down here." Upon the director's arrival the City Solicitor said, "Take that picture off the wall – that is an order." He complied and in a matter of hours there was an uproar all over the country about censorship, with repercussions in Europe, especially in Paris. But the Mayor stood his ground.

The first time I met President Truman was when the Mayor and a group of us went to a $100 a plate dinner in Washington that was a fundraiser for the Democratic Party.

President Truman sat at the center of the long head table shaking hands with a long line of diners who passed along in front of him as did our group. When the mayor reached out to shake the President's hand, Mr. Truman said: "Tommy, I've been reading about you in the papers and I congratulate you on doing a fine job." Then the Mayor introduced me.

My first visit to the famous Oval Office occurred when the mayor persuaded Maryland's entire congressional delegation plus Governor Lane to go with him to ask the President's help with funds to build a new access road to Friendship International Airport, then under construction. I was included in the group.

The President made Federal funds available for a new highway into the airport replacing the country lane then leading to the site.

Subsequently, the Mayor asked President Truman to be the guest of honor when the airport was officially dedicated in June, 1950.

Mr. Truman, knowing of Mr. D'Alesandro's fear of flying, as did most of officialdom and the general public, said he would dedicate the airport but only if the Mayor would fly with him in the Presidential plane from Washington.

Faced with this demand the Mayor agreed to make the first flight of his life for the occasion.

When the big day arrived the mayor, accompanied by Neil McCordell, the City Comptroller, and yours truly rode over to Washington in the official limo and were ushered into the Oval Office where Mr. Truman was at his desk signing some papers. Shaking hands all around, the President joined us in the drive to the Presidential plane. When we were aboard no one could have been more solicitous than was Mr. Truman when he saw that the Mayor was rather nervous. Throwing his arm around the Mayor's shoulder he said don't worry, it's going to be all right. Then the President said he was going to have the pilot fly us around the countryside a bit. This done, we headed for the new airport. It was only a short hop and as we were coming in for a landing the mayor exclaimed that he could see a gang of reporters who would be curious to know his reaction to his first flight. He scored a big hit with the newsmen when upon alighting he said he felt like one of the Wright brothers.

Getting away from the Presidential and back to life at City Hall, it was brought to the Mayor's attention that the need to satisfy the golfing public's hopes for an additional public golf course might be solved by a new course at Loch Raven.

Golf had grown so much in popularity that the four municipal courses were very crowded, but to build a new public course was simply out of the question within the city. On the other hand, although the location was in Baltimore County, the city owned a vast area sur-

Mayor D'Alesandro led a group to visit President Truman in the Oval office consisting of Governor Lane and the entire Maryland Congressional delegation. The author was the last man on the right in the photo. Mr. Truman complied with their request for Federal funds for a new road to Friendship airport, now known as B.W.I..

rounding the huge lake known as the Loch Raven Reservoir. The views around the lake are really great and it was apparent that a sensational course could be created there at a supportable cost since the city already owned the land and only a relatively small portion of the acreage would be needed.

The Mayor recognized the need for a new course so he wrote to the Board of Recreation and Parks that he wanted a new course created at Loch Raven. The city Department of Public Works, which controlled the Reservoir area, endorsed the project.

It was estimated that a bond issue of $500,000 would be needed to build the course, so at the annual combined meeting of the Board of Finance commissioners and the Board of Estimates it was brought up along with other bond issue proposals. I was standing behind the officials where the reporters, who knew of the administration's interest in the proposal, could see me. When it came up for consideration one of the Finance Commissioners, who might have been related to Mr. Scrooge, growled, "Next they will be giving them riding horses." I grabbed my necktie and pulled it over my head as if I were hanging myself and the reporters broke out laughing. The bond issue was voted down but funds were found in the budget to get the project started.

While on the subject of golf, Irving Schloss, the professional at Mount Pleasant, let it be known that he was going to leave the post and move to Florida. Without delay I went to the mayor and told him that my brother, John, still pro at a Virginia country club, was very much interested in the Mount Pleasant position. The Mayor knew John, having met him at several of the Eastern Open tourneys so he said, "As far as I am concerned the job is his but I'll have to get Park Board concurrence." Then he sent off a letter to the Board strongly recommending John for the post. The Board concurred and John served as pro at Mount Pleasant until he retired twenty-seven years later.

One day Jack Pollack, one of the Mayor's strongest political backers, called the Mayor and asked if he could get my help on a matter of importance to him. The Mayor said it was all right with him if it was all right with me. So, we met for lunch and he told me that the political science class at Johns Hopkins University had invited him to speak at an assembly on how one becomes and remains a political "boss-leader," and would I write a speech he could deliver. I told him I would give it a try and for the next hour or so he detailed for me what he does daily the year round to win the support of voters and the cooperation of those whom he helps get elected to office. "You have to help the needy with food, jobs or money," he said, "You have to be patient when you get late night calls from people in trouble. In short, you have to earn the right to ask people to vote your way on Election Day." He said a politician must treat his elected persons with respect and not to call on them to do anything that goes against their conscience. Pollack expressed satisfaction with the finished product I gave him.

The newspapers were informed by Johns Hopkins about the political leader's coming address and his performance got a good write up in the newspapers. Elated with the results, he wanted to know what he owed me and I told him it was on the house.

Another bit of extra curricular activity on my part came from the union of transit employees. They wanted to gain some public support for their demands for higher pay and better working conditions. With the Mayor's OK, I undertook, for a nice fee, to get some favorable publicity for the transit employees. I created a sort of competition called "Transit champ of the month" in which passengers on the busses were asked to vote for the most courteous and considerate bus driver they encountered in any given month. Passengers were asked to ascertain the name and number of their favorite driver and then write or phone it in to the union office. Each month's winner was to receive a watch presented by the union president in a paid commercial on television.

The Mayor continued to have occasional episodes of depression. At times his sparkling personality prevailed and he was at his most energetic and optimistic best. Then he would slip into a depression from which it might take a couple of weeks to shake off. It was early in 1954 that the situation took a more serious turn. He slid into a deep depression from which it seemed he could not emerge. His doctors were trying all then known remedies for what had been diagnosed as a chemical imbalance, and decided that it would be beneficial to treat him in Bon Secours hospital.

As time went on, stretching into months, the Mayor's staff and other city officials performed their routine duties and the President of the City Council, Arthur B. Price, served as Acting Mayor as provided in the City Charter.

Frequent visits were made to the Mayor at Bon Secours and sometimes there would be flashes of his old self but he had lost much weight and progress seemed slow.

Ultimately, the president of the City Council decided to invoke another provision of the City Charter that stipulated that if an elected Mayor became permanently incapacitated then the President of the Council would, de facto, become Mayor. To thwart this, if possible, a statement was prepared for the mayor's signature dismissing Mr. Price as Acting Mayor and stating that Mr. D'Alesandro would resume his duties as Mayor on the following Monday morning. Without much preliminary, the Mayor read the statement and at the urging of one of his brothers, who was visiting him, Mr. D'Alesandro signed the statement. This was on a Saturday evening with plenty of time to make the Sunday papers. "D'Alesandro Fires Price" was the front page headline on the story by William F. Zorzi in the Sunday American. The Sun also carried a big front page story on the event.

THE RETURN FROM ELBA

On Sunday morning Tom Biddison set up a meeting for later in the day at Bon Secour Hospital. In the course of the meeting, which was limited to Mr. Biddison, Hugo Ricciuti, the Deputy City Solicitor, and the Public Relations Director, the hospital authorities and the Mayor's doctors were notified that the Mayor's departure from the hospital would occur at 8:30 AM on Monday morning.

The Mayor faced the coming ordeal with resolution but was understandably a bit nervous about the "Return from Elba." When we arrived at the hospital at 8 AM on Monday, July 11, 1954, the Mayor was all dressed and waiting. Over a cup of coffee we decided how the Mayor and his little entourage would make our entrance to City Hall. The Mayor's offices are on the second floor and we thought it likely that the reporters and photographers would be gathered in the main ceremonial office. So, it was decided we would enter the building by the outside steps, go to the Mayor's small working office by its back entrance so that the Mayor could be sitting at his desk when the press was called in. "Well, here goes," the mayor said as we started up the steps, but he had a big smile and a wave for an enterprising photographer at the top of the steps. When he was sitting comfortably in his old familiar chair at his old familiar desk the reporters and photographers were called in. The City Hall press representatives all liked Mr. D'Alesandro and they seemed delighted that he was back.

In the ensuing weeks the Mayor courageously faced up to his responsibilities and reported to his office every morning and carried out his duties. As the months went by he steadily improved in health. He regained weight and more importantly regained his old vigor and optimism. Pretty soon he was up to beginning preparations to run for reelection to a third term in the spring of 1955 election.

His opponents in the 1955 primary included, of course, Arthur B. Price, the President of the City Council, the man who tried to take the Mayor's job while he was ill. Others in the Democratic primary included Barton Harrington, a well known attorney; Francis X. Dippel, a northeast Baltimore political leader and several others who received scant support. In the Republican primary were Samuel Hopkins, a noteworthy civic leader; William F. Laukaites, an attorney and police court magistrate, and Louis R. Milio, who had been a primary candidate in the 1951 election. The primary fight was pretty hot and heavy at times. Price was putting on a strong bid and Bart Harrington was campaigning vigorously.

Right in the middle of the race a telephone call from Hollywood was routed to me. It was from a representative of a popular weekly television show, "The Name's the Same." The show had a panel of contestants who tried to match the name of a current celebrity being featured on the show with that of someone else of importance in the country.

The query from Hollywood was whether Mayor D'Alesandro would be willing to serve as the "mystery person" on the show. I told the caller the Mayor would want to appear on the show but that because of the political campaign it was doubtful that he could spare the time to go to California right now.

We could come to Baltimore and tape his participation, I was told. Then I was asked whether the Mayor had any unusual routine that could be featured on tape. I remembered that the mayor was shaved every morning in a little barber shop just a block from City Hall. "That's just the kind of thing we want," the Hollywood caller exclaimed. "We'll tape him right in the shop while he's being shaved. We'll have his face covered with lather and then we'll reveal his face and identify him as the barber removes the lather."

His counterpart in Hollywood was a member of the Los Angeles fire department named D'Alesandro who had made a heroic rescue of a child and was to be honored on the show. The Mayor was a little doubtful when I told him about what was proposed but then he started to laugh and said, "Let's do it." I quickly broke the news to the Hollywood caller who was waiting on the line. Sal Cicero, the mayor's barber, was informed of the fact that his little shop was to be featured on national television, and so was the press. There was a crowd

The return from Elba. Mayor D'Alesandro, after months in hospital returns to City Hall. From left Hugo Ricciuti, Deputy City Solicitor, the Mayor, Tom Biddison, City solicitor and Tom O'Donnell.

around the shop and in it as well when the Hollywood people arrived and cheers went up as the mayor was lathered up and then revealed.

The whole affair was a great success, so much so that Bart Harrington complained that it wasn't fair that the mayor received so much local and national publicity. The mayor's opponents credited me with having the stunt set up, but the whole thing originated in Hollywood.

ELECTION A BIG SUCCESS

When the primary election day arrived, the mayor scored a smashing success, receiving 80,370 votes compared with Price's 28,054 and Harrington's 23,036.

In the general election which followed, the Mayor defeated his Republican opponent, Sam Hopkins, by a comfortable margin of more than 25,000 votes.

The day after the election the Mayor received a letter from Gary Black, a principal owner of the Baltimore Sun saying "Congratulations Tommy, you win." Enclosed was a check for a sizeable amount for an addition to the Baltimore Zoo.

GARBAGE STRIKE

The following year, 1956, saw no recurrence of illness but the Mayor and thousands of other Baltimoreans experienced a severe headache ... the sanitation workers (garbage collectors) went out on strike.

The workers, affiliated with the Teamsters' Union, wanted a large increase in pay and drastic improvements in working conditions so expensive that the city administration felt that compliance was out of the question. After lengthy negotiations, the sanitation employees decided that a strike might end the stalemate but after a few days a crisis began to develop. The Mayor and other city officials met in lengthy night sessions trying to find some way to end the impasse. Two weeks passed, garbage kept piling up and a very serious health problem loomed on the horizon. The public was being heard from in no uncertain terms.

It was on a Friday night after a long fruitless session that a suggestion was made by me to the mayor that he issue an immediate ultimatum that any garbage collector who is not on the job ready to work on Monday morning will be fired and under no circumstances will be rehired. This is exactly what President Ronald Reagan did years later to end the air controllers' strike. The proposal to end the garbage strike in this fashion was met by immediate outcrys from the lawyers and others present. ... it would cause irreparable harm, the strike would go on for months, etc. Mayor D'Alesandro spoke out and said, "I like it. Draw me up a brief statement. I will sign it, then notify the press."

The very next morning, Saturday, a national officer of the Teamsters' Union arrived from New York and told the mayor, "Mr. Jimmy [Hoffa] directed me to tell you he is very unhappy with what you are doing. You go back and tell Mr. Jimmy I am very unhappy about garbage piling up on the streets of Baltimore and I am not going to stand for it" the Mayor said. When Monday morning came most of the strikers were on the job and continued negotiations over a period of weeks led to a peaceful and reasonable settlement, and the city administration heard no more about strikes.

The year 1957 saw the earlier mentioned Civic Center controversy; and 1958 was a very exciting period in more ways than one. For example, the Mayor designated me to represent him on a five-day trip to the World's Fair in Brussels, Belgium. This came about when the Mayor received an invitation from British Overseas Airways to participate in their initial flight from Baltimore to Brussels. Although he had flown with President Truman he was not about to make a trans-Atlantic flight, even though the entire trip was expense free. "Would you like to make this trip?" he asked me. I told him I sure would, so he directed me to write a reply designating me as his representative.

While this was a pleasant diversion for me, 1958 turned out to be a hectic time for the Mayor.

He seriously contemplated running as a candidate for governor and he and I made a couple of exploratory trips to Western Maryland and to the counties adjacent to Washington where he consulted with the local party politicos.

He received friendly encouragement wherever he went but also was told that Millard Tawes, the current State Comptroller, had been quietly building political groups throughout the state for his own candidacy. Soon thereafter he received overtures from the Tawes camp urging him to run for U.S. Senator on the Tawes ticket, promising him 100% support in campaign fund raising and in all other aspects.

Reluctantly he agreed and went on to win the Democratic Senatorial primary. This pitted him against the Republican, J. Glen Beall, with whom he had enjoyed a close friendship for years dating back to the time they had served together in the Maryland Congressional delegation.

The Mayor lost that Senatorial election to Senator Beall by only 12,000 votes in a race in which more than 300,000 votes were cast. When Mr. D'Alesandro made the telephone call conceding the election to Mr. Beall they both shed a few tears, he said.

Having lost for the first time in 23 elections, the mayor debated whether he should try for a fourth term as Mayor. To prepare for it he would have only about three months and to raise the necessary funds would be very difficult since he would be going to the well for the third time in less than a year. Reluctant to bow out after his first and only defeat, he decided to give it one more try. He was up against a powerful ticket of opponents already in the field. Running as the "3G ticket," it consisted of Harold Grady, an up and coming lawyer, for mayor; Philip Goodman, a City Councilman, for President of the City Council; and Dr. R. Walter Graham, the incumbent City Comptroller. There probably were a number of factors involved that led to another first for the Mayor, the first loss of a primary election.

For me, it was time to look for another job. I was 48 years old and there was no time to lose. I had never been out of work a day in my life and I didn't want to experience that now. One of my last tasks as public relations director was to make a speech representing the Mayor at the ceremony marking the completion, at long last, of the Pine Ridge Golf Course at Loch Raven, a project dear to my heart. In the speech I recalled the letter from Mayor D'Alesandro to the Park Board stating that he wanted a public golf course built there. He deserved the credit.

Thereafter I found employment in the public relations department at the C & P Telephone Company. I said my goodbyes to the Mayor who still had a month or so to go before surrendering office. I didn't want to be around for that. But as matters turned out it wasn't too long before the Mayor and I teamed up again. This time for another eight years at the Federal level. My work at the highly disciplined telephone company was rather prosaic compared with the hectic times at City Hall.

After about a year I moved on to employment as public relations director for a Baltimore advertising agency. While there, I edited an employees' monthly magazine for the Stainless Steel Company of America and handled publicity for several of the agency's clients.

I was thus engaged for several months when I received a telephone call from my former boss, Mr. D'Alesandro. He asked if I could stop by his house, that he needed my help. I had visited him on Christmas mornings to exchange gifts since he had left City Hall, just as I had done for years and we had kept in touch from time to time. When I got there he asked if I would write a letter for him to the newly elected President John F. Kennedy. It seemed that he had worked actively in Kennedy's campaigns and he expected more or less that Kennedy would offer him a position in the new administration. In fact, there had been stories in the Baltimore newspapers that Mr. D'Alesandro might be appointed Federal Housing Commissioner. Speculation on this had continued in the newspapers and then someone else had been named to the post.

The Mayor, for I still referred to him as Mayor, said he wanted to point out to Jack Kennedy that he had heard nothing from the White House before or after the Housing Commissioner stories appeared in the newspapers and that it had been humiliating that expectations about the appointment proved false. Agreeing with the Mayor that he had a good grievance, I suggested that a letter to the President might not even reach his notice but that a telegram might have more chance. So, we concocted a very long telegram to attract as much attention as possible. Within 8 hours of sending the telegram the Mayor got a telephone call from a member of the President's staff asking if he would be interested in appointment to the Federal Contract Renegotiation Board. He told the caller that he would consider it and would respond in a day or two.

Mr. D'Alesandro obtained a Federal publication that listed Presidential appointments, what the duties were, what the salary would be and other information. Studying it, he learned that the Renegotiation Board consisted of five members and headed an agency that employed numerous accountants, financial and business analysts and lawyers, plus clerks and stenographers. He also learned that each board member had a "special assistant" as well as office staff. The special assistant was rated a GS 15, the highest grade level in the Federal Government except for "Super Grades" of top government officials.

Calling me on the phone, the Mayor said he thought he would accept the appointment and asked whether I would come along with him as special assistant. He noted that the pay was much better than I received at City Hall.

I asked what the agency did and he explained that it recovered excessive profits from defense contractors. He also said that in just a few years the agency had recovered more than a billion dollars in excess profits.

TWO TOMS REUNITED

It sounded good to me so I said I would accept the offer and give the advertising agency notice right away. My wife, Florence, received the news with her usual keen interest and calm acceptance. In all of our 57 years of marriage we never quarreled about such matters. When I made this latest move our older son, Tom, Jr. was 19 years old and a pre-med student at Johns Hopkins University and our younger son, Frank, was 10 and attending Maryvale School, then co-ed, in Baltimore County.

At that time we had been living on Radnor road, in the Govans area, for more than 15 years in a small but very attractive house. Because we had bought an additional lot our back yard extended to the next block and my wife and I had transformed it into a park-like area. With the help of son Frank and nephew, Billy, we created a goldfish pond with fieldstone. In the center of the pond there was a small fountain that kept the water fresh for the fish swimming about. Large bushes on both sides and at the bottom of the yard created a quiet green haven enhanced by lilacs, flower beds and wisteria. I mention these things because when the FBI investigated me for the Federal position my neighbors gave me a good report and said my activities consisted mostly of playing golf and working in the yard. It was in the back yard that we held a family party when son Tom was graduated from the University of Maryland Medical School. Getting back to our new jobs, before taking office the Mayor and I drove over to Washington and were briefed by the agency's general counsel.

TOMMY MAKES A HIT

When we did move in, the new Board member quickly made a big hit with all of the employees of the Renegotiation Board. At his sparkling best, the Mayor went from office to office in our six floor building, shaking hands with every employee in the agency. No Board member in the history of the organization had ever done anything like that. Mr. D'Alesandro told them that neither he nor his special assistant knew anything about the work of the agency and that he was counting on them to teach us. He gave the same message to his col-

Mr. D'Alesandro and staff when a member of the Federal Re-Negotiation Board in Washington.

leagues on the Board.

Basically, whether a contracting company was enjoying excessive profits was determined by the use of common sense. Comparison of prices and profits among government contractors and those in the civilian market for the same or similar products or services was made where possible.

The Renegotiation Board had staffs of competent accountants and business analysts to study annual reports and tax returns of contractors and then make recommendations to the Board.

Often it was desirable for Board members and staffs to visit shipyards and aircraft factories to inspect work in production and check finished products.

Something as commonplace as army shoes and their prices faced comparison to workmanship with civilian market products.

Big refunds came from the big products, aircraft, warships, tanks and other motorized vehicles. Sometimes they involved material costs or overstated hours of labor involved.

During the eight years we worked together at the Renegotiation Board, the mayor and I commuted together by motorcar on our daily trips to and from Washington. In the course of these trips the mayor liked to talk about the old days when he was growing up in Little Italy, so I obtained a tape recorder and preserved many of these recollections.

Years later I typed up the material and took it to the managing editor of the Evening Sun and asked whether the paper would be interested in publishing the stories. There was an enthusiastic response and the newspaper graciously carried the memoirs in five long articles as the much promoted "Tommy's Tapes," and also printed, along with photographs, not only the articles but a commendatory article in a booklet for distribution at a party celebrating the Mayor's 80th birthday. The Sun also carried an editorial headed "Tommy's Tapes," in which the memoirs were described as "a delicious account of a remarkable career."

But the paper wanted more than what it described as "the fleeting mention of his usual balmy, often tempestuous, nearly always educational days as Mayor. Tantalizingly absent," the editorial stated, "is any reference to the problems, personal and political, which he faced and courageously conquered during his first two terms. The nervous exhaustion from which he fought back just in time, barely surviving a swipe at the jugular by a pack of political bosses turning on him in his preelection hour of distress. Or his efforts to cope with the first modern strike by municipal employees in 1956. It is all still there waiting to be told." This book provides much of the information the editorial called for.

The Mayor's service as a member of the Renegotiation Board came to an end in 1969 when a new President, Richard Nixon, was elected. He did not reappoint Mr. D'Alesandro and this did not come as a surprise, Mr. Nixon being a Republican and the Mayor, a Democrat. With the experience I had gained as the Mayor's special assistant I obtained appointment as a business analyst and remained an employee of the Board. During the last three years of my time with the agency I was elected by my fellow employees annually as president of Local 2872 of the American Federation of Government Employees and was honored by the new Board with a luncheon when I retired in 1978 at the age of 67.

When Mr. D'Alesandro departed from the Renegotiation Board he had no thought of retiring. Instead, in April, 1971 he was appointed by Governor Marvin Mandell as a member of the State Board of Parole and in 1972 was re-appointed for a term of 8 years. In an article written as a foreword in the booklet, "Tommy's Tapes," Carl Schoettler, Sun papers reporter, said "There's never been a last hurrah for 'Old' Tommy D'Alesandro," noting that the former Mayor was hard at work as a full-time member of the Parole Board. "Everyone calls him Mister D'Alesandro at the board meetings. He's like an old lion in a pack of cubs. He dominates the room," wrote Mr. Schoettler.

During my last year at the Renegotiation Board I came up with an idea that received international attention. It was a proposal that a united Ireland become the 51st American state and once and for all end the perpetual war between the Protestants and Catholics in Northern Ireland.

The campaign was kicked off with an article written by reporter Robert Blatchley in the Baltimore News American on July 26, 1978. "Thomas J. O'Donnell, of Towson, has had a clay pipe dream for more than a year," he wrote, "so much so that he filed papers with the State Department of Assessments and Taxation, forming a one man Corporation."

"The articles of incorporation state its name as 'Ireland, 51st American State Foundation, Inc.' It's going to take a century to bring something like this about, but it is possible," O'Donnell said. Mr. Blatchley continued with a further quotation: "The admission of Ireland to statehood will not seem incongruous when compared with

Florence and Tom O'Donnell enjoying retirement days, 1988.

statehood for distant Hawaii and Alaska," O'Donnell believes. "O'Donnell has written every U.S. Senator, urging them to co-sponsor a resolution asking President Carter to authorize a study commission on the possibility of statehood for Ireland," wrote Mr. Blatchley. He also noted that I had written to Queen Elizabeth and to various governmental officials in both the Irish Republic and Northern Ireland on stationary bearing the 51st American State logo.

The Baltimore Sun carried an article on its editorial page headed, "The Green State," as follows: "A man must be patient to undertake, on the verge of retirement, a cause he admits will take 100 years to bring to fruition. Patient or a bit zany. Take Tom O'Donnell, former war correspondent , former public relations man for Tommy D'Alesandro the Elder, employee of the Federal Renegotiation Board. His cause is the fifty-first state of the union. Puerto Rico? No. American Somoa? No. Ireland! That's right, Ireland, the Emerald Isle, land of the leprechaun. Tom O'Donnell is promoting the cause of Irish statehood. I'm not sure people will take me seriously," says Tom O'Donnell. "It's far-fetched. I've incorporated a non-profit foundation that's registered with the state of Maryland. So it looks quite official."

"So it does," the editorial article continues. "We got a letter from the Ireland 51st American State Foundation ... announcing a statehood drive both here and in Ireland. Statehood," it said, "possibly could bring about a settlement of the distressing differences, religious and economic between the people of northern Ireland. The letter further explained that the people of Ireland share the English language and the love of freedom with all Americans and would probably feel quite at home with the millions of Irish-American citizens of the United States." The editorial article concluded with the following: "The mind swims at the thought of statehood for Ireland. But, with a name like O'Donnell , what can you expect." The article was signed by John B. O'Donnell, Jr., who happens to be the son of my cousin, John Brophy O'Donnell. These news articles and letters to newspapers in Belfast, Dublin and London kicked off a good deal of trans-Atlantic publicity."

The Dublin Sunday Independent's Michael Riordan telephoned from Dublin and subsequently wrote a friendly article headed, "51 State Plan is Long Term."

The London Sunday Observer, tongue-in-cheek, carried an article headed, "Ireland U.S.A." The Diary Editor wrote: "Now I'm not suggesting for a moment that Thomas J. O'Donnell's new, non-profit corporation, Ireland 51st American State Foundation, Inc. of Edgeclift Road, Towson, Maryland, is a silly corporation. It is merely that O'Donnell has been gathering views from the Queen, Ulster Secretary Roy Mason, Eire Prime Minister Jack Lynch about the possibility of the six countries of Ulster joining Eire to become the 51st State of the Union. "Now why did nobody else think of that?"

The Irish News and Belfast Morning News carried a lengthy letter from me and also listed my address.

The Belfast Telegraph Reporter carried a 3-column article under the headline: "Come Over and Join the U.S. Call to Irish" also giving the Towson address.

"An Irishman's Diary" in the Irish Times carried a substantial part of my letter to that paper and concluded with suggestion that those who wanted more information should write to me at 8 Edgeclift Road, Towson, Maryland.

The article in the Dublin, Belfast and London papers brought a cascade of letters mostly from northern Ireland, strongly supporting the idea of the 51st State.

But articles in such American newspapers as the Chicago Tribune, the Washington Star, the Washington Post and the more than one hundred papers scattered around this country carrying the syndicated column of Dr. Max Rafferty brought a flood of requests for a bumper strip I created to spread the word concerning the 51st State.

The widely read column of Dr. Max Rafferty, the former head of California's Dept. of Education, reached papers in Texas, New Jersey, Montana, Washington, Tennessee, Ohio, Mississippi, Florida, Missouri, Pennsylvania, Massachusetts, Wisconsin, Oklahoma, and other states as well. His column summed up the 51st State proposal saying, "The tip of my hat and the top of the morning, Tom O'Donnell. May I be a stone in your new foundation, Erin go Bragh! Number Fifty-One!" I'm afraid that my proposal, now dormant, may never come to pass, but millions of people read about it and it kept my interest and kept me busy for a couple of years.

When we all were retired, Mayor D'Alesandro, Bill Zorzi, and Bill Pyne, City Hall reporters at the News-Post and Evening Sun, respectively, and I, would have lunch at the famous Haussner's Restaurant and talk over the hectic days at City Hall, every month or so.

Haussner's was so popular it had a no reservations policy but when Bill Zorzi would telephone and say that the Mayor was coming in there would be the "Mayor's Table" waiting for us. He would be greeted by Mrs. Haussner and personally ushered to the table. As he proceeded along he would hear greetings of "Hi Tommy" and "Way to go Tommy" from a sizable percentage of the diners and he would respond to them with a big smile and a wave.

When "Tommy" passed away from a heart related ailment at the age of 84, on Sunday, August 23, 1987, his demise brought about a tremendous outpouring of state and city officials, political friends, and political opponents for his funeral services at St. Leo's in Little Italy.

It was a tribute to a personality and a doer who will be remembered when others are long forgotten.

He lived to see his son, Thomas D'Alesandro III, become Mayor of Baltimore and would have been equally proud of his only daughter, Nancy, who subsequently was elected to Congress from California as Nancy Pelosi, her married name. Congresswoman Nancy Pelosi is now the first woman in history to be elected a minority leader in the U.S. Congress.

My life in retirement was quiet when compared with that of previous decades. Florence was also retired after years as a secretary with the State Department of Education. She had returned to work after both of our sons had grown up.

Every morning before breakfast, I would be off with my dogs, Chief, a beautiful Samoyed, and Fluffy, a chubby mixed breed, for a walk around the perimeter of the Mt. Pleasant golf course, the scene of the now almost forgotten P.G.A. Eastern Open Golf Tournaments, which were dropped soon after the Mayor and I departed City Hall.

Many afternoons in good weather Florence and I were to be found in our secluded backyard, she pursuing her hobby of decorative sewing and I reading from the fine collection of books from the splendid Towson public library.

We were now living in a big old stone house on Edgecliff Road in Towson Estates. We were contented, financially secure and in good health.

Our first born son, Tom Jr., had served his medical internship at Grady Memorial Hospital in Atlanta, was recruited by the U.S. Air Force as a flight surgeon with the rank of Captain and served in Southeast Asia during the Viet Nam War. After his military service he trained as a specialist in orthopedic surgery and practiced in Fresno, California until his retirement. He was married to Gail Coursey, a nurse, and they had two children, a son and daughter, who live in

Young Nancy D'Alesandro, now Congresswoman Nancy Pelosi, of California, highest Democrat in the House of Representatives, enjoys a laugh at a party in the D'Alesandro home. To her right are golf pro John O'Donnell and the author.

Mayor D'Alesandro and young Tommy, 3rd, later to become Mayor himself, on a harbor inspection tour.

Fresno, Melanie Dorian and Matt O'Donnell.

Our younger son, Frank, named for his grandfather, attended Loyola High School, as did his brother and then continued his education at Columbia University for two years and then switched to Princeton, graduating magna cum laude. Following a master's degree from American University in Washington, D.C., Frank embarked on a journalism career and won an Emmy as a news producer at Channel 5 television station and subsequently was editor and publisher of a monthly Washington magazine. He now is Executive Director of the Clean Air Trust, an environmental organization with headquarters in Washington. He is married to the former Mary Norton, a public relations expert with a strong background in print and TV journalism.

Things were too good to last and after a few years they didn't. Florence was hit with colon cancer. She had to suffer through four major operations and after a three- year battle, died on February 16, 1997 at the age of 84 years.

Not very long before that tragic event, my son, Tom, Jr. and his wife Gail had moved to a large waterfront home on Eastern Bay, Talbot County, on Maryland's Eastern Shore.

So Tom and his brother Frank were able to be with me when we drove Florence to Stella Maris Hospice in Baltimore where, at least, she could spend her final weeks in appropriate surroundings.

Tom and Gail wouldn't hear of me living alone in the Towson house where Florence and I had lived for 27 years and insisted that I sell the house and move to the Eastern Shore with them and that is where I wrote this book.

They marked my 90th birthday by throwing me a big birthday party, which was attended by family members in large numbers.

I was very pleased and appreciative.

ORDER FORM

PEARCE PUBLISHERS, INC.
P.O. Box 4923
Timonium, MD 21094
toll free: 1-800-662-2354

Ship to:				Bill to: (if different than shipping)			
Name				Name			
Address				Address			
City	St.		Zip	City	St.		Zip
Day Phone ( )				Day Phone ( )			

Quantity	Title/Author	Price Each	Total Price
	91 Years Down The Road	$14.95	
	With Tom O'Donnell Sr.		

Did you remember to?
√ Print your Name, Address, Zip code & phone #
√ Enclose payment or charge account number
√ Signature for charge order

Subtotal	
Sales Tax	
S & H	
Total	

Enclose your money order or personal check or fill in charge card information below.

   Money Order   Personal Check

   MasterCard   Visa

Exp. Date

Account#

Signature

Shipping Schedule
All orders shipped UPS.
No. P.O. Boxes.
USA shipments only.

Cost	S & H
up to $15	$3.95
$16-$45	$6.50
over $45	call

Mail order to: Pearce Publishers, Inc.
P.O. Box 4923, Timonium, MD 21094 1-800-662-2354

ORDER FORM

PEARCE PUBLISHERS, INC.
P.O. Box 4923
Timonium, MD 21094
toll free: 1-800-662-2354

Ship to:			Bill to: (if different than shipping)		
Name			Name		
Address			Address		
City	St.	Zip	City	St.	Zip
Day Phone ( )			Day Phone ( )		

Quantity	Title/Author	Price Each	Total Price
	91 Years Down The Road	$14.95	
	With Tom O'Donnell Sr.		
Did you remember to?		Subtotal	
√ Print your Name, Address, Zip code & phone #		Sales Tax	
√ Enclose payment or charge account number		S & H	
√ Signature for charge order		Total	

Enclose your money order or personal check or fill in charge card information below.		**Shipping Schedule** All orders shipped UPS. No. P.O. Boxes. USA shipments only.	
Money Order	Personal Check		
MasterCard	Visa	Cost	S & H
Exp. Date		up to $15	$3.95
Account#		$16-$45	$6.50
Signature		over $45	call

Mail order to: Pearce Publishers, Inc.
P.O. Box 4923, Timonium, MD 21094 1-800-662-2354

RELEASED FROM CIRCULATION

Donated by the
Wayne Civitan Club
to the
Wayne Public Library
Children's Collection

Read All About Sharks

THE SHARKS' WORLD

Lynn Stone

The Rourke Corporation, Inc.
Vero Beach, Florida 32964

© 1996 The Rourke Corporation, Inc.

All rights reserved. No part of this book may be reproduced or utilized in any form or by any means, electronic or mechanical including photocopying, recording or by any information storage and retrieval system without permission in writing from the publisher.

PHOTO CREDITS
©Marty Snyderman: cover, p.4, 9, 10, 12, 16; ©Herb Segars: p.6; ©Tom Campbell: p.7, 15; ©Mark Conlin/INNERSPACE VISIONS, p.13; ©Mark Strickland/INNERSPACE VISIONS p.18; ©Lynn M. Stone: p.19; ©Wayne and Karen Brown: p.20; © Doug Perrine: p.22

Library of Congress Cataloging-in-Publication Data

Stone, Lynn M.
   The shark's world / by Lynn M. Stone
     p. cm. — (Read all about sharks)
   Includes index.
   Summary: Briefly describes where some species of sharks live and how they catch their food.
   ISBN 0-86593-444-4 (alk. paper)
   1. Sharks—Juvenile literature. 2. Predatory marine animals—Juvenile literature. [1. Sharks.]
I. Title II. Series: Stone, Lynn M. Read all about sharks
QL638.9.S8495 1996
597'.31—dc20   96-7967
                                                                                                     CIP
                                                                                                     AC

Printed in the USA

TABLE OF CONTENTS

The Sharks' World 5
Habitats 6
Habits 8
Senses 11
The Marine World 12
Shark Prey 14
Shark Teeth 17
Shark Enemies 18
Ancient Sharks 20
Glossary 23
Index 24

THE SHARKS' WORLD

The sharks' world is the ocean. Sharks live in all kinds of oceans—shallow, deep, warm, and cold. The big Greenland shark, for example, lives in icy Arctic water.

Most sharks never leave the ocean. The bull sharks of South America, though, sometimes swim into freshwater rivers.

Sharks are perfectly designed for ocean life. The long, streamlined bodies of most kinds of sharks glide easily through warm water.

The sand tiger shark is a powerful predator in its ocean world.

HABITATS

The Earth has more than twice as much water, or ocean, as land. Within those oceans are many different **habitats** (HAB uh tats), or kinds of ocean homes for animals. Sharks of one kind or another live in almost all of those habitats.

The Caribbean reef shark hunts the coral reefs of the Caribbean Sea.

Flat as a flounder, a Pacific angelshark lies hidden in the ocean sands.

Some shark **species** (SPEE sheez) or kinds, live in deep, dark water. Others like the warm, clear, shallow water over coral reefs. A few sharks are at home on the ocean bottom. They lie hidden in the sand.

HABITS

Some species of sharks are much more active than others. Sharks such as the blue, tiger, mako, and great white are very active fish. They sometimes travel long distances.

A shark may have to travel for food. Some sharks also travel to find a comfortable water temperature.

Some sharks lie almost motionless at the ocean surface. Others lie quietly for long periods on the ocean bottom.

A prowling great white shark passes underneath a diver's boat.

A blue shark feeds on swarms of reddish, shrimplike krill in the Pacific Ocean.

Many of the plant-eaters, in turn, are gobbled by meat-eaters, like blue sharks. Some of the smaller meat-eaters are eaten by larger ones.

SHARK PREY

You may imagine sharks to be the mightiest predators in the sea. Along with killer whales, some of them are. Most sharks, though, are not as long as you are tall. That means that some sharks don't have as big an appetite as you might expect.

Great white sharks are truly tigers of the sea. They eat seals, sea lions, and marine turtles. Some sharks eat much smaller prey—fish, squid, shrimp, sea urchins, and even **plankton** (PLANK ton).

Plankton is made up of tiny, floating plants and animals.

The huge whale shark, largest fish in the sea, eats plankton and small fish.

SENSES

Ocean **predators** (PRED uh terz), or hunters, must catch other animals, their **prey** (PRAY), to survive. A shark's senses help it locate prey.

Most kinds of sharks seem to have good eyesight and a great sense of smell. In experiments, sharks knew if even one part tuna juice was added to 25 million parts of seawater.

Sharks also do well in their underwater world because they can sense the slightest sounds and movements.

Cruising sharks can locate prey through sight, smell, and even slight movements in water.

THE MARINE WORLD

Sharks share the **marine** (muh REEN), or ocean, world with many other creatures. Some of the creatures are prey for sharks.

All creatures in the marine world depend upon the sun for survival. Tiny marine plants change sunlight into food. The tiny plants become food for countless, plant-eating animals.

Sunlight powers the lives of plants and animals in the undersea world.

12

SHARK TEETH

Being a predator means having weapons to kill. A shark's main weapons are its teeth.

Most sharks have pointed, razor-sharp teeth. Some have sawlike edges. A few sharks, however, have flattened teeth for crushing small, hard-shelled creatures.

Shark teeth break off quite easily. A shark gets around this problem by always having teeth in reserve. A shark can have five or more sets of teeth present at the same time.

Open jaws of mako shark reveal rows of long, razor-sharp teeth.

SHARK ENEMIES

Even with jaws full of sharp teeth, most sharks have at least a few enemies.

Small sharks can be attacked by larger ones. Even sharks of the same species will dine on each other.

Porpoises sometimes kill sharks, and sharks sometimes kill porpoises.

Large adult sharks have almost no enemies, except the spears, guns, hooks, and nets of people.

Porpoises (shown here) sometimes dine on small sharks. Sharks sometimes dine on porpoises, too.

The largest sharks, though, really have no enemies, except people. The only marine predator that could tackle a large shark is the killer whale, or orca. As far as anyone knows, that has not happened.

ANCIENT SHARKS

The marine world has been the habitat of sharks for millions of years.

Sharks of one kind or another have probably been around for 450 million years. One of the ancient sharks, dating back just 10 million years, was the huge megalodon. It may have grown to 50 feet.

The megalodon had teeth longer than seven inches. In comparison, the longest teeth of great white sharks are just over two inches.

The largest teeth of ancient megalodon sharks were much larger than the teeth of any modern sharks.

GLOSSARY

habitat (HAB uh tat) — the special kind of place where an animal lives, such as an ocean coral reef

marine (muh REEN) — of or relating to the ocean

plankton (PLANK ton) — tiny, floating plants and animals of the sea and other bodies of water

predators (PRED uh terz) — animals that hunt other animals for food

prey (PRAY) — an animal that is hunted by another animal for food

species (SPEE sheez) — within a group of closely related animals, one certain kind, such as a *Greenland* shark.

Nurse shark rests on a shallow Bahamas coral reef.

INDEX

coral reefs 6
enemies 18
eyesight 11
food 8
habitats 6
ocean 5, 6
plankton 14
plants 12
porpoises 18
predators 11, 14, 17
prey 11, 12, 14

rivers 5
sharks
   bull 5
   great white 14, 20
   Greenland 5
   megalodon 20
senses 11
sunlight 12
teeth 17, 18, 20
whale, killer 14, 19